JOHN EDGAR PLATT

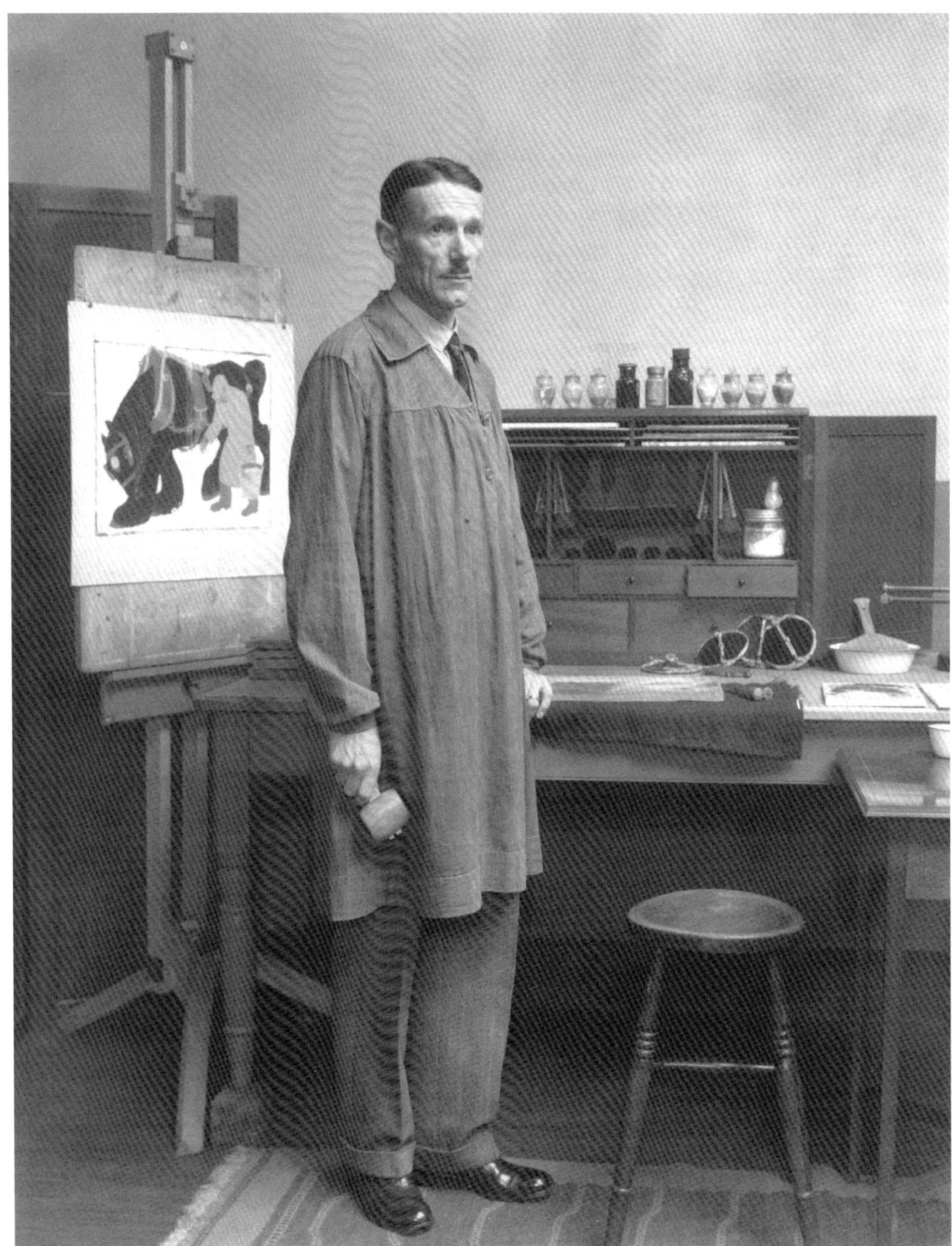

JOHN EDGAR PLATT

Master of the Colour Woodcut

Hilary Chapman

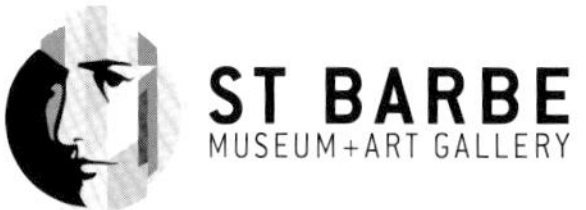

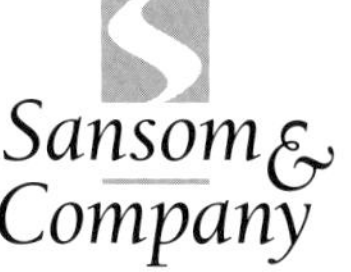

First published in 2018 by Sansom and Company,
a publishing imprint of Redcliffe Press Ltd.,
81G Pembroke Road, Bristol BS8 3EA
www.sansomandcompany.co.uk / info@sansomandcompany.co.uk

Text © Hilary Chapman
Images © Estate of the Artist (unless otherwise noted)

Published to coincide with the exhibition
'Colour Cuts: woodblock prints by John Edgar Platt and Allen William Seaby'
at St Barbe Museum and Art Gallery, Lymington,
29 September–25 November 2018

ISBN: 978-1-911408-30-7

British Library Cataloguing-in-Publication Data
A catalogue record for this book is available from the British Library.

Design and typesetting by E&P Design
Printed and bound by Cambrian Print, Aberystwyth

Front cover: *Mullion Cove*, 1931
Frontispiece: John Edgar Platt in his studio

Contents

Introduction

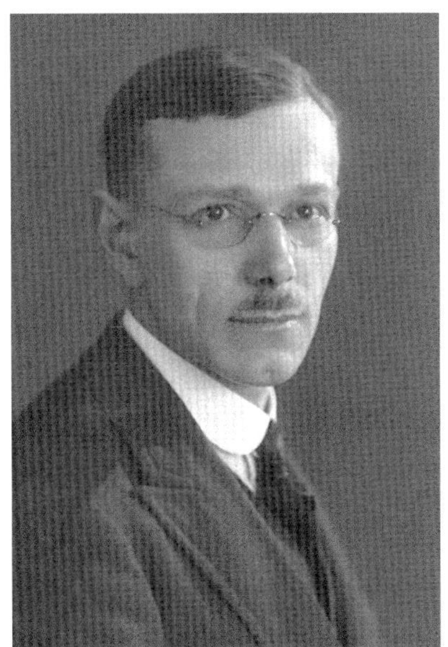
John Edgar Platt

The inter-war years saw a remarkable flowering of British printmaking across a range of media. These were the last days of the so-called etching revival before the lucrative market for such prints vanished with the Wall Street Crash. The Society of Wood Engravers was formed in 1920 and some of Britain's most notable artists of the time including Paul Nash, Eric Ravilious and Eric Gill excelled in the medium. The Grosvenor School of Modern Art was responsible for a brief but intense flourishing of the colour linocut.

The colour woodcut is less celebrated than the aforementioned forms of print but also underwent a renaissance in the early-twentieth century with a number of societies, articles and instruction books appearing to promote its appeal. Colour woodblock prints made in the Japanese manner by John Edgar Platt, Allen William Seaby, Frank Morley Fletcher and others are perhaps the most notable in this medium and have an enduring charm.

This book provides an overview of the life and work of John Edgar Platt as well as a catalogue raisonné of his work as a printmaker that ranges from early Arts and Crafts influences to the more modernist compositions of the late 1930s marked by pared-back and simple design geometric forms. It is intended to complement existing publications on his friend and fellow wood-cut printmaker Allen William Seaby and has been produced to accompany an exhibition of both artists' work at St Barbe Museum and Art Gallery.

Both book and exhibition would not have been possible without the help of a number of individuals and organisations and in particular we would like to thank Hilary Chapman who has expanded on her previous work on Platt to provide insightful essays on his life and technique as well as full details of the individual prints. We would also like to thank the artist's estate for giving us access to so many of Platt's prints and allowing us to reproduce them. For their help in developing the exhibition and publication we are also most grateful to Martin Andrews, Elizabeth Axford, Robert Gillmor, Clara Hudson, Emma Mackinnon, Jackie Millard, Ian Parfitt and Susanne Platt.

Steve Marshall
Exhibitions Curator
St Barbe Museum and Art Gallery

John Edgar Platt and the British colour woodcut

John Edgar Platt (1886–1967) was a gifted painter, designer and craftsman, but he is best remembered as an exceptional printmaker. His exquisite prints, executed during the 1920s and 1930s, were produced by colour woodcut using traditional Japanese methods. By adopting these arduous and skilful techniques, which had been used by the Japanese craftsman for centuries, Platt's prints of animals and landscapes beautifully demonstrated the simplified designs and the translucent, gradated, water-based colours of the Japanese colour woodcut. His prints contributed to a popular movement in British printmaking in the early-twentieth century which embraced the modern, the decorative and the colourful. Unlike the dynamic, bright colour linocuts of the now famous Grosvenor School artists who were popular during the same period,[1] Platt's colour woodcuts represented a more intellectual and craft-based approach to modernism in the medium of the colour print. Employed for most of his working life as an art teacher and the principal of several art colleges, Platt believed that skilled craftsmanship was the basis to all art, whatever the medium, and passed on this ethos to his pupils. His work ethic allowed him time to produce his own prints successfully alongside his teaching, and he was also willing to take on the more prosaic tasks associated with promoting the colour printmaking technique that he had adopted with such enthusiasm, as a medium for original printmaking.

Platt does not appear initially to have intended a career as an artist; he was planning to study as an engineer at Manchester University after his school years in Newcastle. However, after a brief period studying at Margate Art College whilst recovering from a minor accident, and encouraged by a tutor who recognised his artistic ability, he changed his mind and decided to study art. He undertook his art education at Margate, Newcastle and Leek Schools of Art and won a scholarship to the Royal College of Art in 1905. This cemented his choice of career and over the next five years he was to achieve outstanding success, not only in the fine arts, but in architecture and design and the crafts of stained glass, poster and book production, as well as tapestry design, metalwork and jewellery, lettering and illumination, wood carving and architectural woodwork. His ability to master these many craft-based skills was an indication of his extraordinary versatility and artistry. Platt had also taken a teaching qualification whilst at the Royal College of Art and in 1910 he took up the post of Principal of Leek College of Art. He was exhibiting regularly at the Royal Academy and the New English Art Club, while undertaking commissions including designs for stained glass and

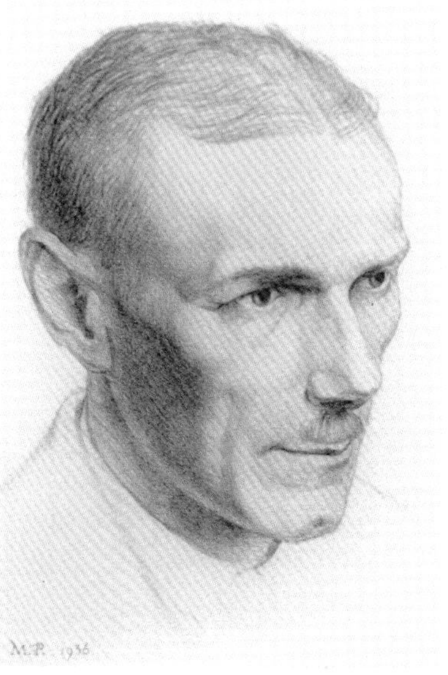

Pencil portrait of John Edgar Platt by his son, Michael Platt
private collection

painted decorations for furniture, ceilings and panelling at Lady Chapel, All Saints Church in Leek.

His marriage to Phyllis Harvey-George (also a scholar at the RCA) took place in June 1911. Her father had run a fleet of herring fishing trawlers out of Gorleston, near Great Yarmouth, and boats and the sea were in Phyllis's blood. The couple always spent their holidays near the coast where they both painted and sketched boat yards and boats of all kinds. In 1912 the couple's daughter Anthea was born, and in 1914 a son Michael. But this promising start to his life and career was interrupted, as for so many artists of this period, by service in the First World War and in 1914 Platt took a commission in the Royal Army Service Corps (Motor Transport).

Just prior to his war service, Platt had become involved with a group of friends and artists associated with Frank Morley Fletcher (1866–1949), director of the Edinburgh School of Art and Allen W. Seaby (1867–1953), director of Reading School of Art. These artists were at the forefront of a new approach to colour woodcut printing which adopted the Japanese techniques of applying water based pigments to the blocks by brushes and then printing the blocks by hand. (In Britain and Europe at this time colour woodcuts were mostly produced using oil based inks, applied by rollers, and printed on presses.) The Japanese technique enabled artists to produce the beautiful effects and colours seen in the woodblock prints which had been imported from Japan in large numbers to Britain and Europe in the late-nineteenth century and were greatly admired by print collectors and connoisseurs.

The artist printmaker, Morley Fletcher, had been studying in Paris in the 1890s when he developed a passion for Japanese prints and an enthusiasm for the technique which he saw had potential for artists wanting to produce original colour prints. After some fairly unsuccessful experimentation in printing from blocks in watercolour with another enthusiast, J.D. Batten (1866–1932), he cast around for information and came across the only source on the technique at this time – a translation from the Japanese of *Japanese Wood-Cutting and Wood-Cut Printing* (1892) by T. Tokuno which was reprinted in *The Studio* in 1894. Very soon Morley Fletcher had imparted his knowledge and enthusiasm to his colleagues Seaby and Walter Crane (1845–1915)[2] at Reading School of Art, to other artists via his classes at the Central School of Arts and Crafts, London and, later, at Edinburgh College of Art where he was Director from 1908 to 1923. Morley Fletcher also published a handbook on the technique in 1916, followed by Seaby who published an extensive article in the *The Studio* in 1919 and a handbook in 1925.[3]

Another important name included in the group of artists who first adopted the Japanese method of colour printing was William Giles (1879–1939). Giles had studied in Paris where he developed an interest in the techniques of the Japanese colour woodcuts. Returning to Reading around the turn of the century, he worked with Morley Fletcher and also became an early exponent of the colour woodcut producing several remarkable prints. His role, not only as a teacher, but as a force in promoting the technique, was instrumental to

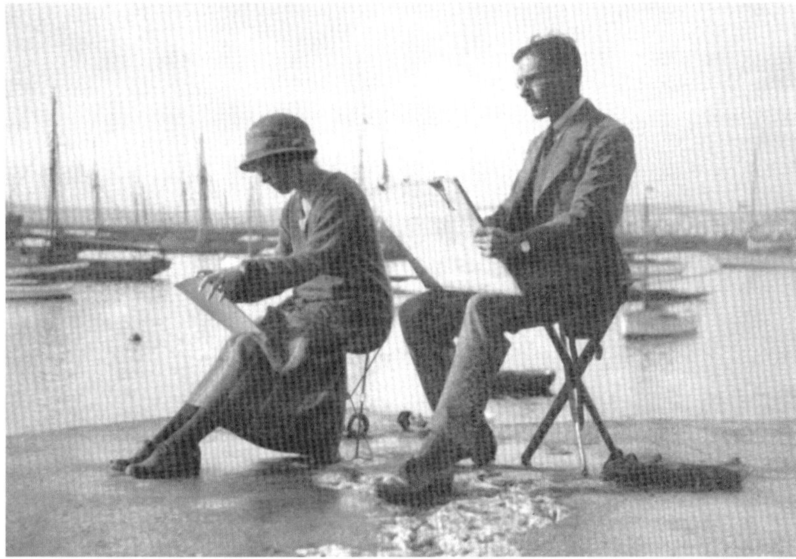

John and Phyllis Platt sketching

the success the British colour woodcut was to achieve for the next thirty years.

Platt had collected Japanese woodblock prints from an early age and, as a craftsman, was also intrigued by the method of their production. So, when he came into contact with Seaby and Morley Fletcher as an external examiner at Reading School of Art, he joined the growing group of practitioners and enthusiasts of the technique, passing on his enthusiasm to his pupils after the war at the art schools in Harrogate and Derby where he was Principal. In 1920, Platt left for Edinburgh to take a part-time appointment at Edinburgh School of Art under Morley Fletcher. A drawing of a picturesque cottage by Platt in the Platt family archive bears the inscription, 'Cottage at Chantemesle where Charles Condor worked 1890–1893 & Fletcher, Seaby and I stayed July 1922'. The later correspondence between the artists is testament to their long lasting friendship.

As well as being an artistic fraternity, Morley Fletcher, Seaby, Giles and Platt all played an important role in the development of the Society of Graver-Printers in Colour (SGPIC) which was formed in 1909. The impetus for the formation of the Society came from the need for any artist to exhibit regularly and to be associated with some recognised establishment. For original print-makers in Britain since the late-nineteenth century, this role was embodied in the Royal Society of Painter-Etchers and Engravers (R.E.) established by Sir Francis Seymour Haden in 1880. The assertion of original prints as a fine art was well established by the first decade of the twentieth century, but this position had become exclusively the realm of the intaglio techniques of black and white etching and engraving; although wood engraving was beginning to

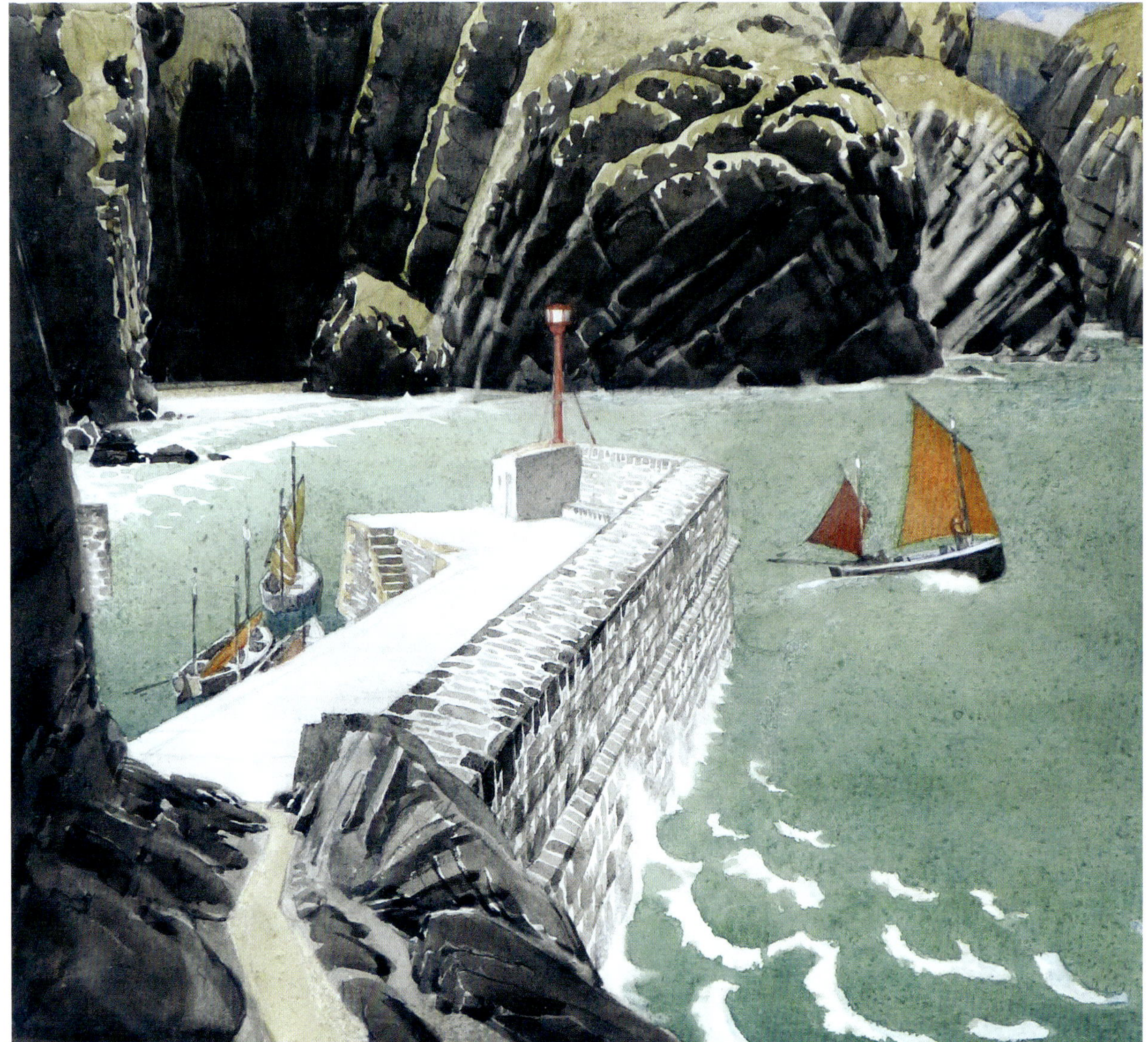

Fully worked up watercolour of Mullion Cove, Cornwall. The subject was used for the colour woodcut, *Mullion Cove* (cat. 20)
private collection

be occasionally accepted. Any print in colour was expressly disallowed.[4] Colour was associated with commercial printing, and colour woodcuts in particular with cheap book illustration. In the purist circles of the twentieth-century etchers, the use of colour had a whiff of vulgarity about it. Several exhibiting societies had sprung up at the turn of the century to give support to the burgeoning number of original printmakers, but the challenge for the group of colour printmakers who gathered in 1909 was to try to circumvent the attitude to their colour prints, and to assert the fact that these prints were also original fine art work. Having experienced the same attitude in France with regard to his colour prints, the French artist and printmaker Theodore Roussel (1847–1926) was involved in the formation of the Société de la Gravure Originale en Couleurs in 1904, which had enabled French artists producing original colour prints to exhibit in their annual shows. Now settled in London, he contacted artists producing colour prints in order to form a similar organisation and, in 1909, the SGPIC was formed with Roussel as President.[5] Shortly after its formation the three artists working with the new form of colour woodcut using the Japanese technique, Morley Fletcher, Seaby and Giles, were elected as members. Other artists working in this medium were soon a substantial part of the membership and, apart from the difficulties experienced during the First World War, this organisation flourished for the next thirty years. The annual exhibition, held at major London galleries, was to become the main showcase for artists producing original colour prints. Further societies also began to appear as the colour woodcut technique gained popularity: The Colour Woodcut Society, formed in 1919 and the Central Club of Colour Woodblock Engravers formed in 1924 which also encouraged the production of colour woodcuts. The popular art magazine *The Studio* also promoted the medium throughout the 1920s and 1930s with numerous articles by writers and critics of repute.

Platt joined the SGPIC in 1928 during the Presidency of William Giles. By this time he had moved back to London and was appointed Principal of Blackheath School of Art – a part-time appointment which he had negotiated in order to continue with his own work. This was a period of much artistic activity for him as he travelled around the country, filling sketch books with drawings and working them up into paintings and prints which were exhibited at annual shows at the RA and the SGPIC and sold through London dealers. The colour woodcuts he produced after the war years developed a true understanding of the Japanese aesthetic and are significantly different from his first known attempt in 1916, *Venantius of Ravenna* (cat. 1) which was strongly influenced by decorative designs of the Arts and Crafts Movement at the turn of the century. Other earlier works demonstrate a skilful use of the technique with beautiful deep and translucent colour, albeit combined with a traditional use of figurative subject matter. A development can then be traced through the prints of the 1920s and 1930s whereby the motifs and spatial aspects of Japanese prints become more apparent with 'birds-eye view' compositions and a simplification of the forms. His later prints of the 1930s such as *Lapwings* (cat. 32)

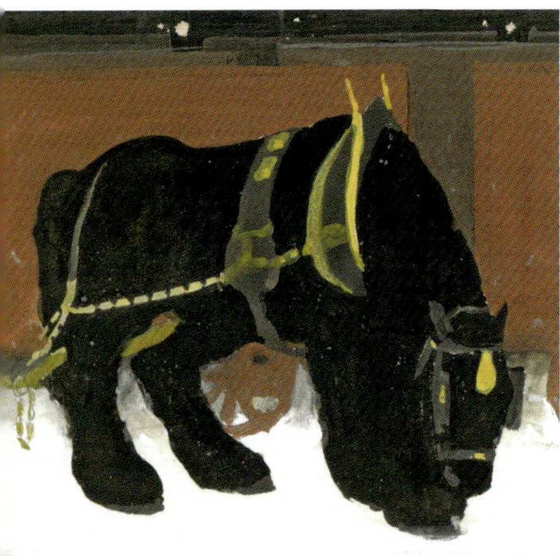

Gouache sketch of a carthorse,
possibly for the woodcut *Horse* (cat. 25)
private collection

and *The Plough* (cat. 33) are strong exemplars of these qualities. He received critical acclaim and was recognised as one of the finest exponents of the colour woodcut, exploiting not only the Japanese technique, but incorporating the formal stylistic qualities of traditional Japanese colour woodcuts into his designs to form a perfect marriage of eastern and western art. As his friend and colleague Seaby remarked, 'There is no doubt that in your hands the wood print has been raised far above its former status.'[6]

Platt's success was only achieved after much endeavour. The craft of the colour woodcut is an arduous process. The woodblock printmakers of Japan had produced their prints in such large numbers by the use of divided labour; the Japanese artist designing his print then giving it to a block cutter, and then to the printers to complete an edition. To design, cut and print his own work, an artist has to spend many hours of concentrated effort. Platt's printing notes and edition books were kept meticulously and bear witness to the number of blocks required to be cut for each print, and the number of printings needed to build up the design. He recorded that he could only print ten prints of an image at one session with some prints requiring up to eight separate blocks.[7] Fortunately Platt could sustain these periods of laborious work and his son, the artist Michael Platt, recalled hearing long hours of mallet on chisel as Platt worked on his woodblocks far into the night.

It is remarkable therefore that Platt found time alongside his own artistic production to inspire, teach and promote the colour woodcut. His overall impact on art education of the period was extensive and his methods and commitment to the melding of an art and craft education influenced a generation of students in the many colleges and institutions where he held important posts. At Leek and Harrogate he introduced courses for Applied and Industrial Art and, whilst Principal at Leicester School of Art, forged valuable links with industry, believing strongly in the necessary interplay between a School of Art and local trade crafts. His own teaching was rigorous and, as befitted his personality, kindly but firm. He was described in his obituary in *The Times* as, 'a teacher and organiser of worth. Very much the schoolmaster in manner, precise in speech and tidy in habits.'[8] He always responded positively to requests for lectures or articles and included his thoughts on the practice of the artist and printmaker in a series of articles he wrote for the magazine *The Artist* from the March until the September issue in 1934. Earlier, in 1924, he delivered a lecture to students where he commented on his perception of the modernist aspect in contemporary colour woodcuts; a view demonstrated by the stylistic development in his own prints: 'The effects most readily expressed in woodblock printmaking are just those which have always interested the artists of the Far East, that is emphatic expression of the subject by the selection and arrangement of essentials and the suppression of all that is irrelevant. It is interesting that this method as perfected by the Japanese has now become available for Western artists just at a time when its particular character is in accord with the current ideas and aims of Western art.'[9]

Platt was also aware of the importance for students of experiencing practical demonstrations of the craft of the colour woodcut, particularly if the printmaker was a master who could provide the finest examples of work to which the student could aspire. Undoubtedly, at this time, it was the Japanese artist based in London, Yoshijiro Urushibara (1889–1953), who could provide this experience. Platt had known Urushibara as a friend and colleague for many years and in 1929, when he was still Principal at Leicester College of Art, Platt asked him to come and demonstrate his practice of colour woodcut printmaking. Urushibara's importance in the development of the British colour woodcut is discussed in the following essay, but his wide renown as a printmaker of great repute, trained in the famous firm of Shimbi Shoin in Tokyo, meant that the students could experience and learn from an artist steeped in the traditional skills.

In 1938 Platt also added to the knowledge of the technique of the colour woodcut in the Japanese manner by publishing his own handbook to complement those published earlier in the century by Morley Fletcher and Seaby. Very concise and explicit, it was illustrated by some of his most attractive prints and was well received.[10] That year also saw the beginning of some great challenges in Platt's career. He began to be more active in the SGPIC after becoming Vice President in 1937 during the Presidency of William Giles. On Giles's sudden death in 1939, Platt was voted in as President, with Seaby taking the role of Vice President. Giles's term of office had been highly beneficial to the Society; he had greatly enhanced the profile and importance of the institution and brought the technique of the colour woodcut in the Japanese manner to a wide and appreciative audience; he had forged links with important practitioners in the USA and Europe; he had negotiated the acquisition of many works by colour woodcut artists by the Directors of the British Museum, the Victoria and Albert Museum and other museums and art galleries, and written widely on the subject; and he had also established the Colour Print Club to encourage collectors, and provided subscribers with a journal and a presentation print each year. The Journal contained many informative articles from scholars and practitioners.[11] Unfortunately for Platt, and the Society, Platt's Presidency was to coincide with the onset of the Second World War, a dwindling number of subscribers and members and the Society's eventual demise.

Platt's own production of prints also ceased from 1939, apart from two nautical subjects in 1940 and 1945. He was appointed an official war artist to the Ministry of War (Transport) in 1943 and for the next two years travelled widely producing, drawings, watercolours and oil paintings of the maritime landscape around the coast and of the rivers of Great Britain; his knowledge of boats and shipping from years of sketching and observation standing him in good stead. Many of these paintings were major works and several are included in the collections of the National Maritime Museum at Greenwich and the Imperial War Museum.

Throughout this period Platt had tried hard to keep the SGPIC going but the situation continued to deteriorate. In 1939 Platt had received a desperate

letter from Henry Hayley, the Secretary to the Society for many years:
'... how best can we face the apparently insuperable difficulty against holding
an exhibition, with Walker Galleries at present darkened into the likeness of
a cave and deserted. In the event of holding an exhibition how many of the
members can produce work'.[12] In fact, the Society staggered on, bolstered
by some sales from travelling exhibitions organised by the British Council,
and, with the cessation of war, Platt started to put the Society's affairs in
order and to consider reactivation. With frantic activity, great dedication
and some help from Hayley and Seaby, he managed to contact many of the
surviving members, arrange loans of deceased artists' work and put together
an exhibition at the Art Exhibitions Bureau in South Kensington entitled
'Fifty Years of the Colour Print' which took place in December 1948. The
show was reasonably well attended but received little attention from the
Press. Platt had to accept that the Society, and the popularity of the colour
woodcut, was now in decline. Seaby had expressed concern for the future
of the medium earlier by noting practical problems, such as the difficulties
of acquiring essential materials such cherry wood blocks, Japanese paper
and the lack of teachers for the technique. It had to be recognised that there
was little interest in the medium of the colour woodcut which, in the artistic
environment of the post-war years, was perceived only as a difficult and time
consuming craft. The Society closed its doors in 1953.

In 1949, Platt's wife Phyllis died unexpectedly. Platt's own health
deteriorated and he went to live with his daughter in Eastbourne. The next
period of his life was sadly unproductive artistically, and increasingly limited
personally. He died in 1967. His studio contained many paintings and prints
which were kept intact by his daughter, and later by his granddaughter. More
recently these have been dispersed to collectors and museums and art galleries,
and a new audience has been able to appreciate the work of a true artist and a
remarkable craftsman. Platt's colour woodcuts are a tribute to the techniques
of an ancient Far Eastern craft which he was able to emulate with great skill.
With his colleagues, pupils and many other artist printmakers of the time,
he responded to an external and foreign influence and produced new forms
and a decorative approach to the use of colour. The early-twentieth century
colour woodcut in the Japanese manner occupies a discrete and significant
place in British art.

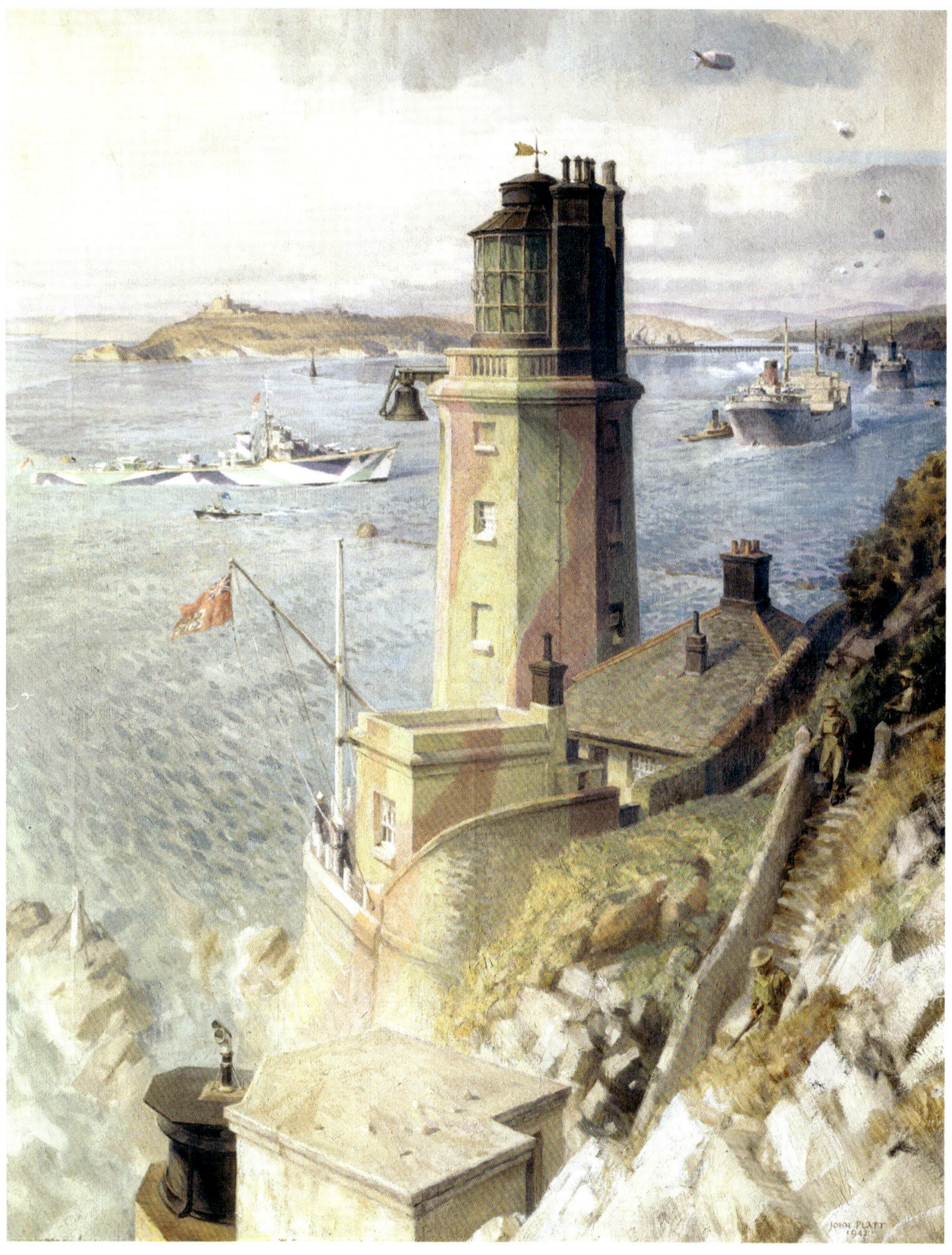

Convoy Arriving off St. Anthony's Lighthouse, Falmouth
1942, oil on canvas, 913 x 710 mm

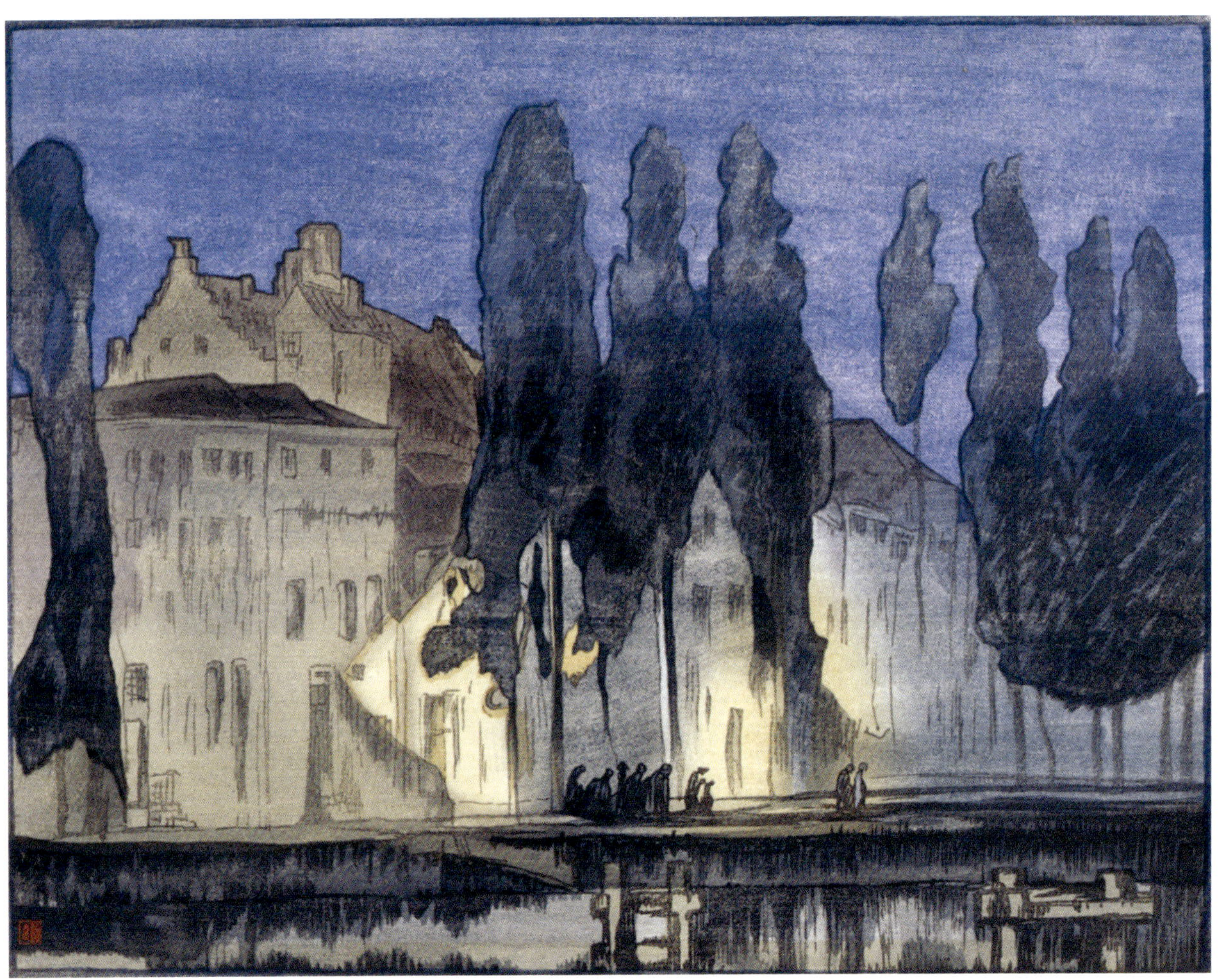

YOSHIJIRO URUSHIBARA (after Frank Brangwyn)
Potterierei, Bruges, 1919, colour woodcut
courtesy Estate of the Artist

The influence of Yoshijiro Urushibara

The art of the Japanese colour woodcut dates back many centuries and reached a peak with the famous Ukiyo-e prints of artists such as Katsushika Hokusai (1760–1849). However, Japanese colour woodcuts and block printed books were only rarely seen in the West until around 1845 when Japan was opened again for trade after a period of over 200 years during which it had been closed to nearly all foreign powers. By the mid-nineteenth century Japanese art and artefacts were being imported to Europe in great numbers and, at the Paris Exposition Universelle of 1867 where Japan first exhibited independently, Japanese art was revealed to a large section of the public. It was met with great enthusiasm and the late nineteenth and early twentieth century became the period of *Japonisme*; the fashionable assimilation of Japanese art and design in the West.

The first group of artists in Britain to take a special interest in the Japanese colour woodcut as a vehicle for original printmaking, and who were eager to find out about the technique, was centred around Frank Morley Fletcher and Reading School of Art. John Edgar Platt became part of this group around 1914 and, after service in the First World War, adopted and developed his own career as a printmaker in colour woodcut. As discussed in the previous essay, these earliest exponents of the colour woodcut had to rely on experimentation and the translations of a few Japanese tracts in order to learn the intricacies of the Japanese technique. Although there were Japanese artists living in London at the beginning of the twentieth century, the group do not appear to have received any instruction from a practising printmaker – that is until Yoshijiro Urushibara (1889–1953) arrived in London.[1]

Urushibara was a member of the group of craftsmen from the Tokyo firm of Shimbi Shoin taking part in the Japan-British Exhibition held at White City in Shepherds Bush in 1910. He was born into a family of craftsmen in Tokyo and received instruction from established colour woodcut printmakers in the time honoured way. At a young age he was employed by Shimbi Shoin where he further developed his skills. The workshop was run on the classic division of labour where each craftsman specialised in an aspect of the finished work. The designer would transfer an artist's image onto a wood block, a carver would cut the blocks for each colour and a printer would prepare paper, apply colour and print the blocks. The workshops of Shimbi Shoin were known for publishing high quality reproductions of paintings by famous Chinese and Japanese artists and Urushibara learned the new techniques, developed at Shimbi Shoin, for mastering the intricacies of reproducing brush strokes

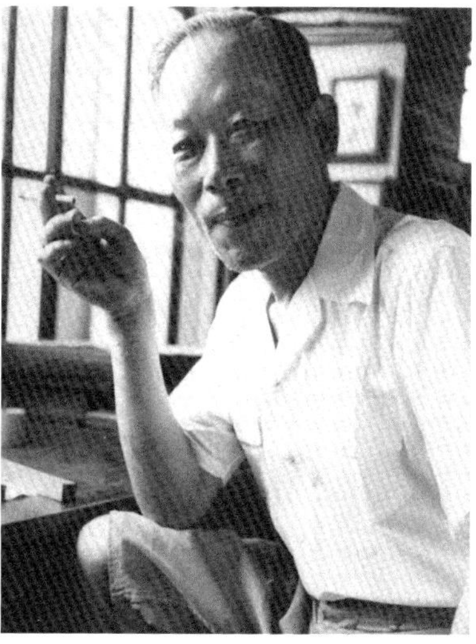

Yoshijiro Urushibara
courtesy Estate of the Artist

and the texture of paint. This skill was to stand him in good stead as,
just as the Japan-British Exhibition was coming to a close in 1910, he was
commissioned to make a colour woodcut reproduction of the famous Chinese
painted handscroll in the British Museum collecton, *Nushi zhen (Admonitions
of the Instructress of the Ladies in the Palace)*.[2] With just one other colleague,
Urushibara stayed in London and completed this project in 1912. His remarkable expertise was duly noted and he was offered a post in the British Museum
as a restorer of old Chinese and Japanese paintings and prints; a position he
held until 1919.

Until the outbreak of the First World War Urushibara travelled across
to France quite extensively, demonstrating the technique of colour woodcut
to artists in Paris. But it was London that became home. Very soon his skills
as a printmaker were beginning to be recognised by British artists, in particular by Frank Brangwyn RA (1867–1956), the renowned painter, printmaker,
muralist and designer. Brangwyn is thought to have met the Japanese printmaker around 1910 at the Japan-British Exhibition when Brangwyn was on the
committee of the Japan Society who helped organise the event. He would also
have seen Urushibara's work at the British Museum and by 1917 he had already
commissioned him to interpret some of his sketches and watercolours as
colour woodcuts. Brangwyn's work was always in great demand and he could
now see an opportunity to produce editions of prints after his works which
were not only in colour, but executed with such skill as to fully interpret and
reproduce his bravura style, replicating perfectly his watercolour brushstrokes
and the vivacity of his drawing. One of the most famous collaborations was
the *Bruges* portfolio of 1919.[3] These collaborative prints revealed the versatility
of the technique in the hands of a master; that such fluidity of colour and
spontaneity of design could be attained by the medium was remarkable.
Lawrence Binyon, in his Introduction to a further collaborative portfolio
of prints in 1924 wrote '... let no one imagine that the translation is easy and
a merely mechanical affair, or that such qualities of tone and atmosphere and
luminosity can be gained without long experience and peculiar skill. Only
those who have seen Mr Urushibara at work can appreciate what such
mastery means.'[4]

Platt was amongst many other printmakers who recognised the Japanese
printmaker's skills and admired the wealth of effects that he could attain in
the medium. He also became a good friend and it is very likely that Platt encouraged Urushibara to develop his creative abilities and to make more prints
from his own designs. Urushibara had made some earlier original prints, and
there is evidence that he attended classes at an art school in London around
1912. One of his first prints, a study of Stonehenge, was added to the British
Museum print collection in 1916 and shows a somewhat stark view of the
standing stones in an empty landscape in simple harmonies of green and
blue. To further encourage the Japanese artist to produce original works,
Urushibara was also invited to join the Society of Graver-Printers in Colour
(SGPIC) and began exhibit with them regularly. He also exhibited at the

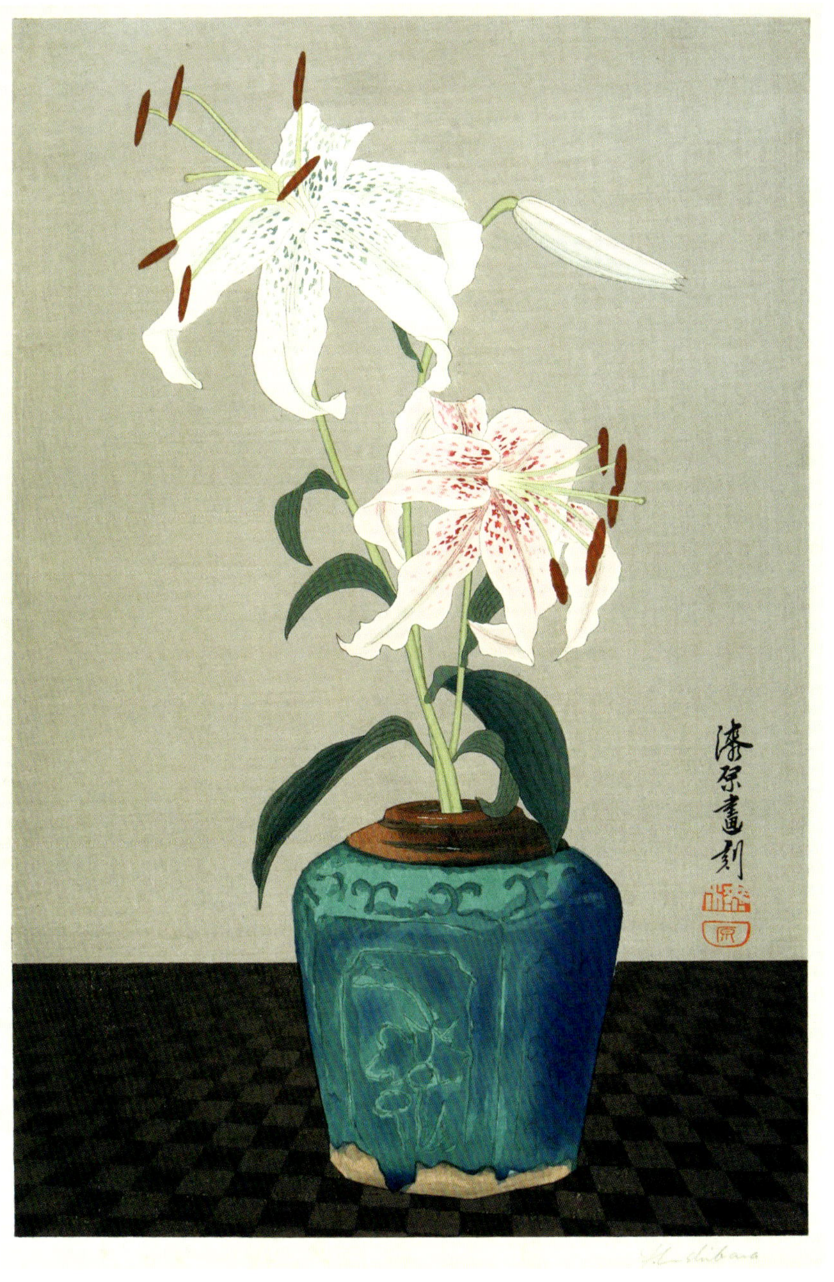

YOSHIJIRO URUSHIBARA
Lilies 1, c.1920, colour woodcut
courtesy Estate of the Artist

Royal Academy and had a one-man show at the Abbey Gallery in London in 1928. His work became popular and was often singled out by critics for its originality and decorative qualities. Although Urushibara chose mostly western subject matter, and particularly the familiar plants of an English garden, he managed to imbue his prints with an Eastern 'flavour'. As in traditional Japanese colour woodcuts, the subjects were depicted with simplicity of form, often without backgrounds and in one plane, and were highly attractive with their exquisite colours and novelty of design. This Japanese design aesthetic, subtly integrated into his prints, no doubt influenced some of the British colour woodcut artists of the period. Platt himself changed his style towards the end of the 1920s to more simplified designs as a possible response to Urushibara's work.

Urushibara served as a Council member of the SGPIC from 1922–1937. His contributions to the Society took the form of dealing with 'Japanese matters' and his articles on technique appeared in Society's journals. He could give much valuable advice to printmakers on the preparation of tools, on trimming and shaping brushes, preparing colours, pastes and the paper used for printing. This information was based on the traditional technique of colour woodcut he had acquired from his rigorous training in Japan. Urushibara made many friends in Britain and he appears to have been generous to a fault with his time; assisting and teaching other artists, providing technical information and, of immense value, prepared to demonstrate the technique to artists, to students and at art classes held for the public around the country. Platt was not alone in acquiring his services when he asked Urushibara to demonstrate to his students at Leicester School of Art.

Tragically for Urushibara, after achieving success with his collaborative and original prints, his life and career in London was to end abruptly in 1940, after the outbreak of war, when he and his family were repatriated to Japan. Platt was President of the SGPIC at this time and his correspondence with Henry Hayley, the long serving Secretary to the Society, indicates their deep concern for Urushibara and their attempts to get the Society to provide assistance, as much of the artist's studio had to remain in London.[5] The following decade was traumatic for the family as resettlement was difficult and, although Urushibara's success in Europe was recognised in Japan, there was little in the way of a market for his prints in war-torn Tokyo. During the war he worked as a clerk for a chemical company and in 1945 returned to his printmaking, mostly providing works for the new market that had sprung up amongst the occupying forces. His health failed and he died in June 1953 of lung cancer.

Platt had recognised Urushibara's importance as an ambassador for his craft and valued his unique contributions to the successful development of the colour woodcut as a fine art in Britain. He had encouraged his production of original prints and helped him to pass on his expertise through articles and demonstrations. He had also gained personally, not only by his friendship with the Japanese artist, but by the stimulus to his own stylistic development from a printmaker who reflected the glorious Japanese tradition.

The colour woodcut in the Japanese manner

As described in John Edgar Platt's handbook, *Colour Woodcuts: A book of reproductions and a handbook of method,* published by Pitman in 1938 for their series entitled 'The Student's Art Books'.

∗

Platt's book was published nearly two decades after Morley Fletcher published the first handbook in Britain on the technique of producing colour woodcuts in the Japanese manner in 1916. Platt's aim was to describe and explain the intricacies of the technique through his own working practices, well established over two decades, and by using his own prints as illustrations. Platt's colour woodcuts had undergone a development in style by 1930, moving away from a more linear design, based on an outline key-block with several colour blocks, to the gradual abandonment of the key-block and the use of fewer blocks with larger masses of colour modulated by tone. This development can be seen in the later prints that he uses as illustration and which demonstrate his understanding of the suitability of the technique for expressing modernist concepts. In his Introduction Platt wrote, 'The colour woodcut has great possibilities for the practising artist, and he may find in it a means of expressing his own ideas and producing works of art of a kind eminently suited to contemporary conditions.'

Very clearly laid out, and with assistance on the descriptions of printing materials and tools from Yoshijiro Urushibara, who he generously acknowledges, the book gives a full and practical description of this complex medium. The foreword by Campbell Dodgson (Keeper of Prints and Drawings at the British Museum 1912–1932) praises Platt for his lucidity: 'In this treatise he expounds the craft of which he is a master with an equal mastery of words.'

The following is a summary of the procedures of the Japanese technique that Platt describes in great detail in the book.

∗

The design to be made into a colour woodcut is first traced onto very thin Japan tissue paper and pasted down onto a block of wood, usually cherry. When the paper is dry the defining outline of the design is cut on each side of the line through the paper. This will constitute what is known as the key-block [sometimes called 'keyline block', Platt uses 'key-block']. All the areas that do not constitute the key-block are pared away. (Where the design has no linear outline, the most significant mass of the design is

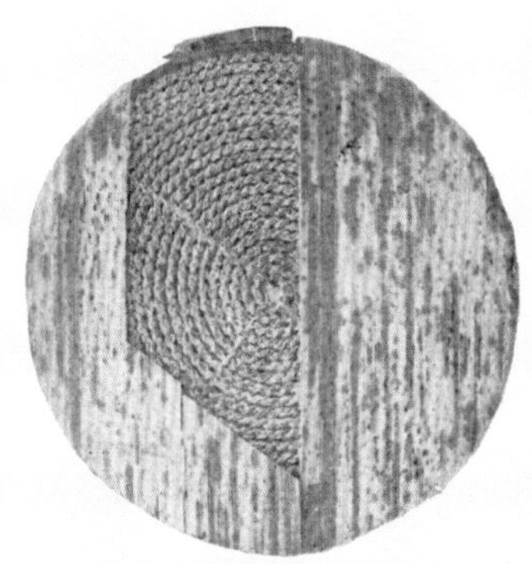

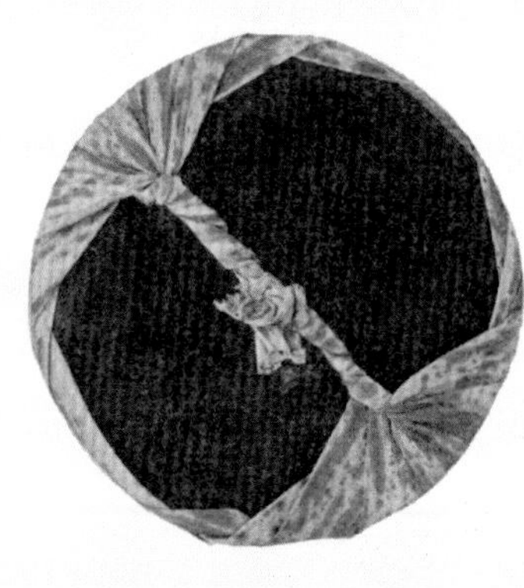

The baren, from *Colour Woodcuts*, p. 19

selected to form the key-mass and used as the key-block.) Register marks in the form of two shallow depressions are cut on the wood block to mark where the paper will be placed for printing, one of these marks is a right angle and the right hand corner of the paper is placed there. The other depression is used to align the bottom edge of the paper. The lines of the outline standing in relief, and the registration marks, are lightly brushed in grey or black ink; Platt used a stick of Chinese ink, broken up, soaked in water and 'mashed' up. Paper is placed on the block to line up with the registration marks and an impression taken from the key-block. Several other impressions are taken from the key-block from which all the other blocks, for each of the colours, will be derived.

To print the colours, one of the key-block impressions is pasted onto another block, and registration marks, identical to those of the key-block, are made. The areas for one particular colour are marked out. The block is then cut to leave just the areas that will be needed to print the colour, with the rest of the block again pared away. Blocks are then cut for each of the other colours. (For his own prints Platt would use five to nine blocks for one print, one for each colour, sometimes cutting on both sides of a block to save wood.) The register marks have to be exactly the same relative position on each block to ensure the key-block and all the coloured areas of the print never overlap. The blocks are coloured by firstly brushing pigment mixed with water onto each block in the designated colour with various size brushes, and then with rice flour paste to help set and control the colour. The brushes have stiff, springy hair and are flat underneath. Using long wide sweeps, great control over tone, and the gradations of the colour over an area can be obtained. To print the design much thought has to go into the sequence of the printing of the blocks. The paper – Japanese paper that has been previously sized and prepared – is then dampened and laid on the first block, usually on to the key-block, which is again brushed lightly with black or grey. The paper is then rubbed from the back using a baren: a thin, rimmed disc of papier mâché into which a coil of tightly-plaited bamboo fibre is fitted and encased in a bamboo leaf. The leaf is cleverly twisted to form a handle at the back. When the baren [see picture, left] is rubbed over the back of the paper more, or less, pressure can be applied as required to increase or decrease the depth of the colour.

Having printed the first batch with just the image of the key-block, usually 10–20 impressions, the other blocks are prepared and the batch overprinted with all the colours in sequence to form the final image [see facing page].

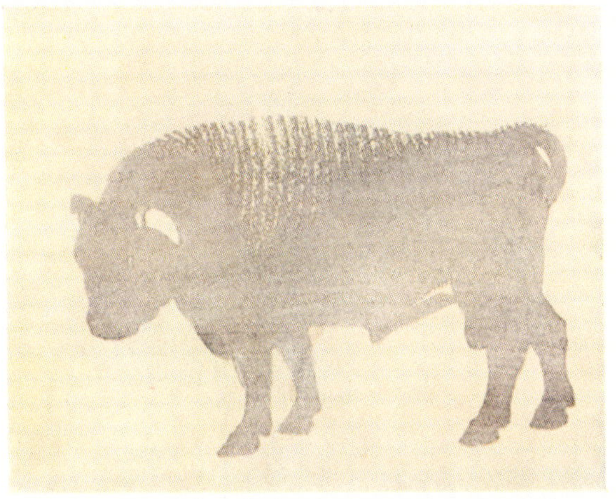
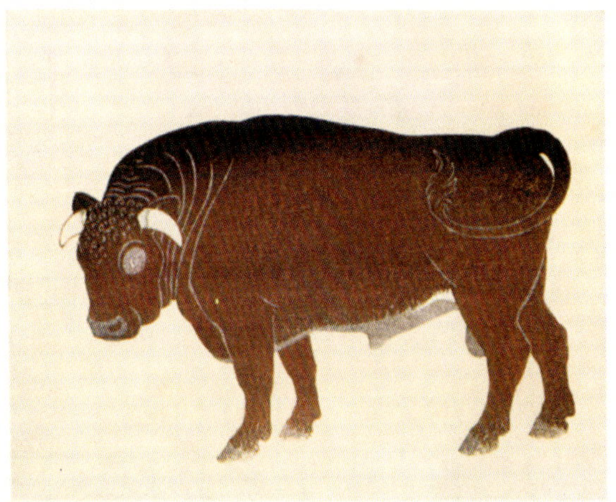
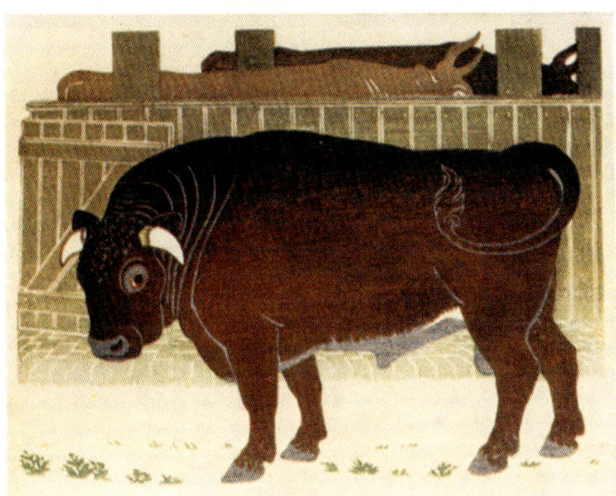
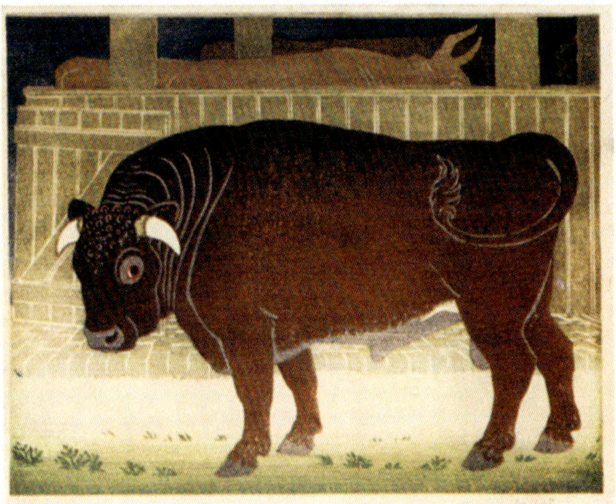

PLATE V

THE RED BULL

Size of each original 9 in. × 11 in. Four stages of printing.
(1) Key-mass (no key-block used). (2) A narrow dark gradation
along the shoulders added, and a flat red tone printed all over.
(3) The eye printed in vermilion and black, then the shippen
and cows added. (4) The print complete.

The Red Bull, four stages of printing, from *Colour Woodcuts*, p. 22

Catalogue

Much of the information in this catalogue has been compiled from John Platt's edition book and printing notes. The printing notes have now been donated by the Platt family to the Print Room at the British Museum. They give detailed and comprehensive information on the artist's working procedures.

Editions: Platt's edition book gives the projected number of impressions for each print executed before October 1930. These projected numbers were rarely achieved. The number of impressions recorded here are taken from Platt's edition book and the printing notes.

Around 1931 Platt ceased to give a projected edition number. He wrote a note inserted in the edition book around 1948: 'No guarantee of (the) number in (an) edition is given by me, instead (I) guarantee that (the) print is cut and printed by (the) artist.'

Platt annotated his prints in the lower margin with a single number, or with a number out of an edition (e.g. 25/100). Some were numbered with Roman numerals, usually denoting that the impression has been printed subsequent to the numbered edition.

Paper: Platt always used Japanese paper of varying thickness for printing the colour woodcuts. Types most frequently mentioned are Torinoko (some with Hosho backing) and Hosho (some tea-stained from his own recipes recorded in the printing notes). Platt printed his impressions in small batches, often using a different type of paper for each batch.

Colours: Platt used a wide range of fine ground powder colours mixed with water. For the rich blacks and various hues of grey in his prints, he used Chinese ink sticks which he broke up, soaked for several days and then mashed to a jelly.

Due to the complexity of Platt's printing procedure, the colours in the prints have been simply listed and do not refer to the sequence of printing. The details of the sequence can be ascertained from Platt's printing notes. The notes also contain samples of the colour mixes used for the earliest prints, and pasted-in swatches cut from proofs for those after 1925.

Central to Platt's work was experimentation and variation in applying colour to the blocks. Impressions of the same image therefore exist in subtle variations of colour. Where the differences in colour are obvious these are designated and listed.

Exhibitions: From 1919 until around 1950 Platt exhibited his paintings and prints regularly in Britain and abroad, as well as sending prints on consignment to commercial galleries in London, Glasgow, Edinburgh and New York. Between 1939 and 1948 his work was also included in exhibitions arranged by the British Council in many countries around the world.

Abbreviations
BM: British Museum
NEAC: New English Art Club (annual exhibitions held at Suffolk Street Galleries, Pall Mall, London)
RA: Royal Academy (annual exhibition)
SGPIC: Society of Graver-Printers in Colour, (annual exhibitions: 1920–1933, Bromhead, Cutts & Co., Cork Street, London; 1934, P&D Colnaghi & Co., London; 1934–1937, Walker Galleries Ltd., London; 1947 Kensington Art Gallery, London)
V&A: Victoria and Albert Museum

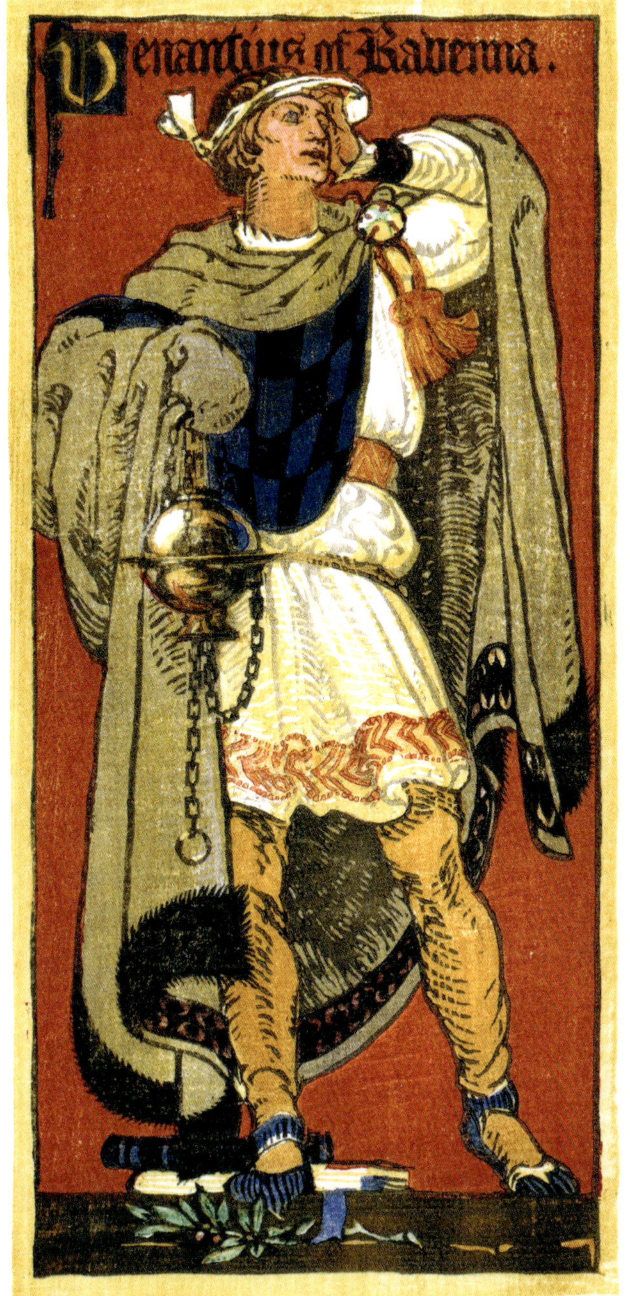# 1 / *Venantius of Ravenna*

December 1916 / 213 x 102 mm

Printed in eight colours on Japanese paper; red, grey, blue, yellow, brown, green, orange, with black key block. Projected edition of 50 (13 recorded, plus some trial proofs).

Literature: *The Studio*, 1917, vol. 72.
Collections: BM, acquired 1918.

This woodcut relates to Platt's designs for a printed panel on an organ case in the Lady Chapel of All Saints Church in Leek, Staffordshire (*c.*1913–1915) entitled 'Venantius Fortunatus'. Venantius was a poet and a songwriter who was cured of blindness. He became Bishop of Poitiers in 599.

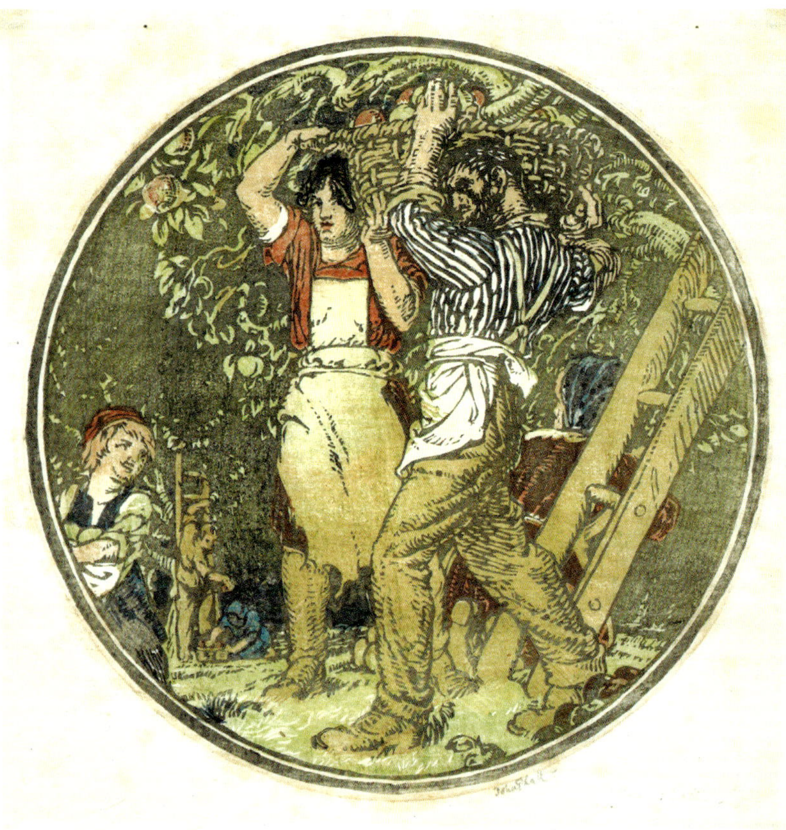

2 / *Apple Gatherers*

Colour
1917 / 165 x 165 mm

Monochrome
First printed 1920 / 165 x 165 mm

Printed in six colours on Japanese paper; red, yellow, green, blue, brown, with black key block. Projected edition of 50 (19 recorded).

Printed in two colours on Japanese paper; light brown with dark brown key block. Projected edition of 50 (19 recorded).

Literature: *The Studio*, 1917, vol. 72.

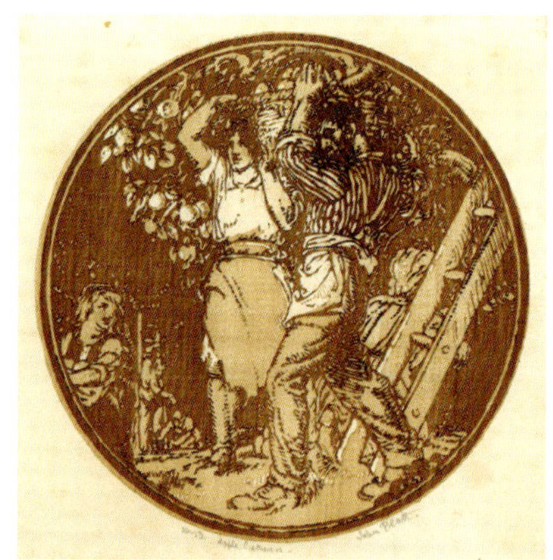

3 / *In Derbyshire near Matlock*

October 1917 / 224 x 221 mm

Printed in five colours on Japanese paper; green, blue, yellow, brown, with black key block. Projected edition of 100 (48 recorded).

Exhibited: SGPIC, 1920, 6th annual exhibition, no. 29; NEAC, winter 1917/18, no. 58.

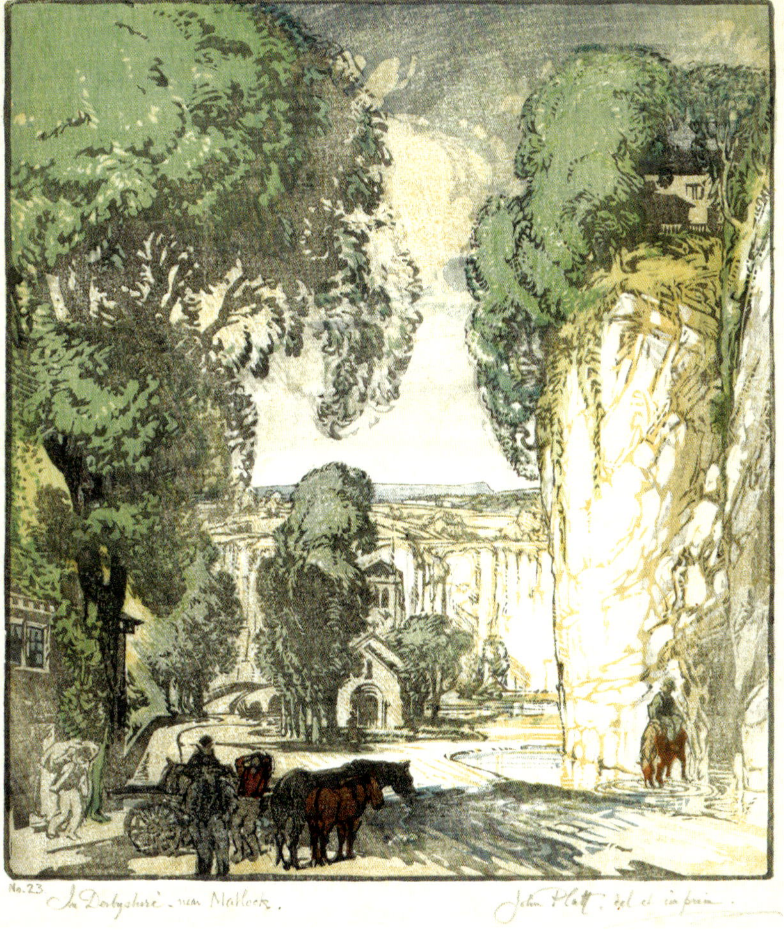

overleaf

4 / *The Giant Stride*

October 1918 / 169 x 410 mm

Printed in eight colours on Japanese paper; blue, pink, red, grey, green, purple, yellow, with black key block. Monogrammed with date centre top. Projected edition of 150 (120 recorded, plus four numbered E1 to E4).

Exhibited: SGPIC, 1920, 6th annual exhibition, no. 30; Los Angeles Museum, Los Angeles, 1922, 3rd International Exhibition (organised by the Printmakers Society of California), awarded a 'Gold Medal' for the best print in any medium.
Literature: *The Studio* (special number), 1919; *Drawing and Design*, November 1924; *The Artist*, April 1934.
Collections: BM, two impressions acquired 1918 and 1932; V&A, acquired 1934; The Pushkin State Museum of Fine Arts, Moscow, gifted by Campbell Dodgson, Keeper of Prints and Drawings at the British Museum in 1926.

Platt states in his printing notes that each impression took eight printings from four blocks cut on both sides. He used sketches of his family to compose this subject. They include (on the swings): 2nd and 3rd from left, Platt's two sisters; baby in the centre, his son Michael; 5th from the left, his daughter Anthea; 6th from the left (boy in blazer), his brother Sidney; 8th from left, his wife Phyllis; figure on the beach with parasol, his mother.

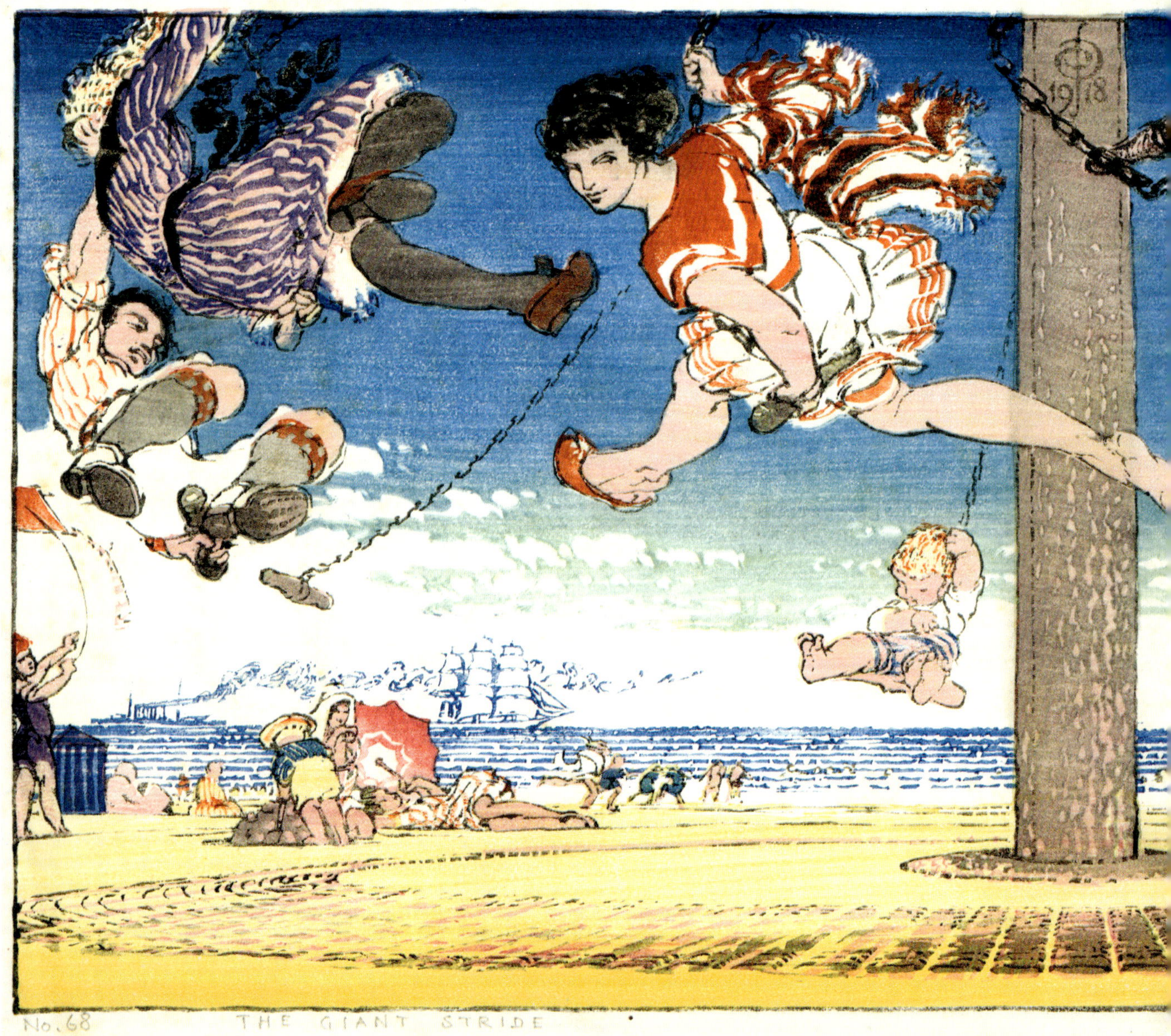
No.68   THE GIANT STRIDE

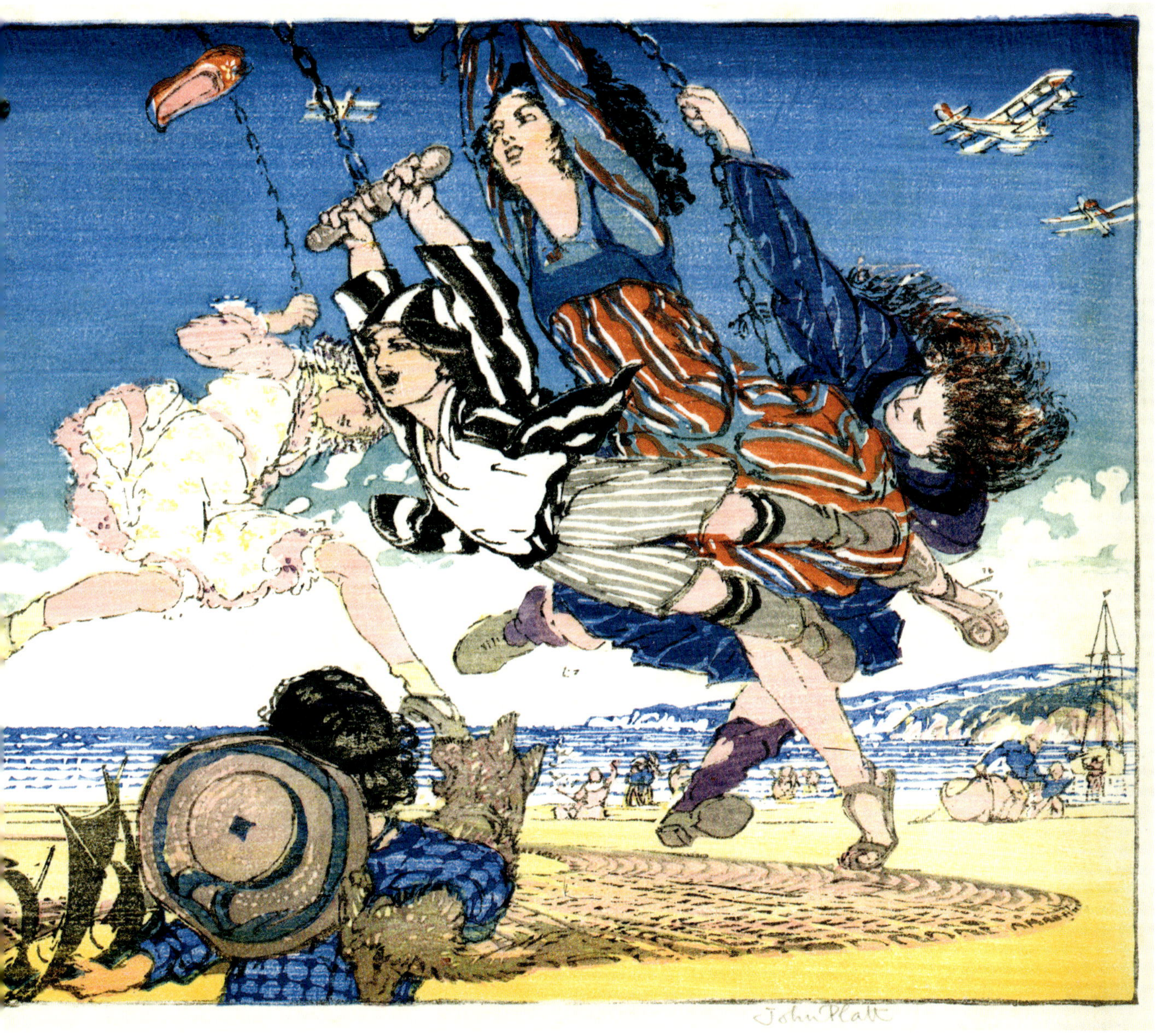

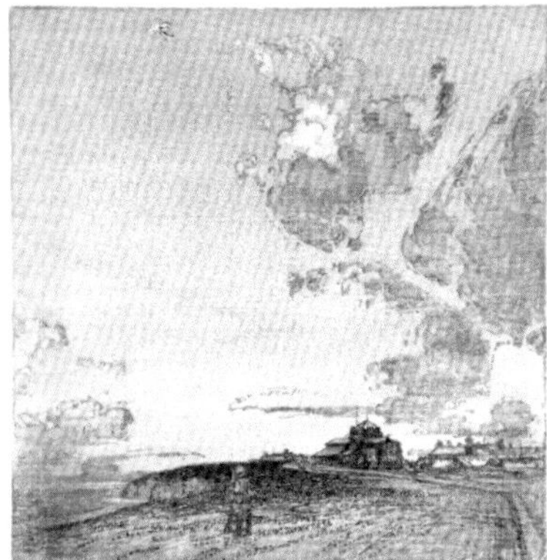

5 / *Dawn*

1918 / 205 x 202 mm

Printed in four colours on Japanese paper; blue, pink, dark grey, light grey. Projected edition of 50 (4 recorded).

Exhibited: SGPIC, 1923, 8th annual exhibition, no. 13.

Platt states in his printing notes that only four trial prints were made of this print as 'the subject was abandoned as too formal in conception for the medium'. However, it should be noted that one impression seen is numbered 6.

6 / *Snow in Springtime*

1920 / 243 x 301 mm

Printed in nine colours in Japanese paper; pink, brown, blue, red, orange, grey, yellow, purple with black key block. Bears monogram and date 1919 lower right. Projected edition of 100 (71 recorded).

Exhibited: SGPIC, 1920, 6th annual exhibition, no. 31; Japan Society of London Tokyo, 1925; IXth Olympiad, Amsterdam, 1928.
Collections: BM, acquired 1920; V&A, acquired 1934.

The models for this composition also relate to Platt's sketches for *The Giant Stride* (no. 4). His sisters are on the swing watched by his daughter and son (in the pram).

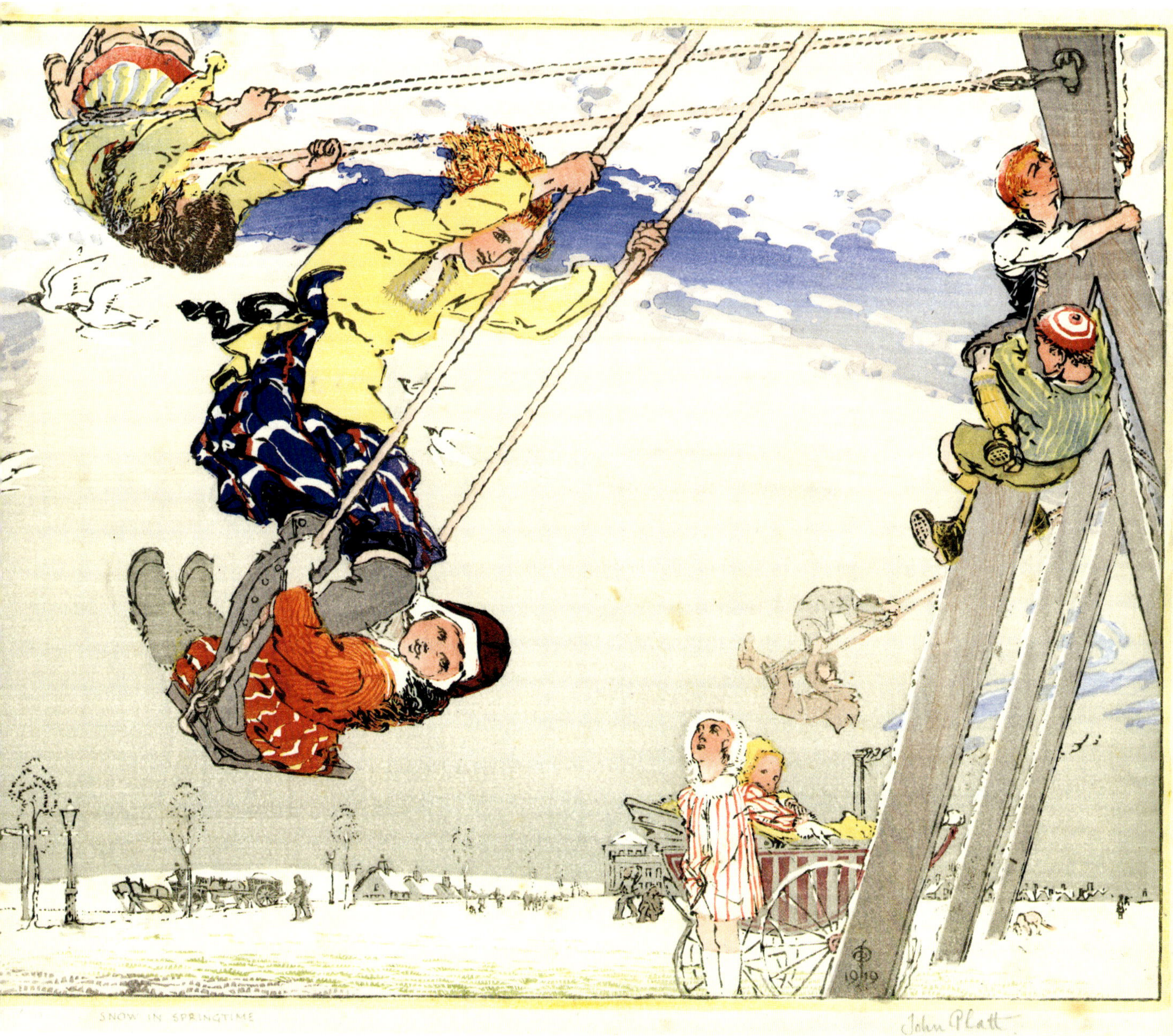

SNOW IN SPRINGTIME
John Platt

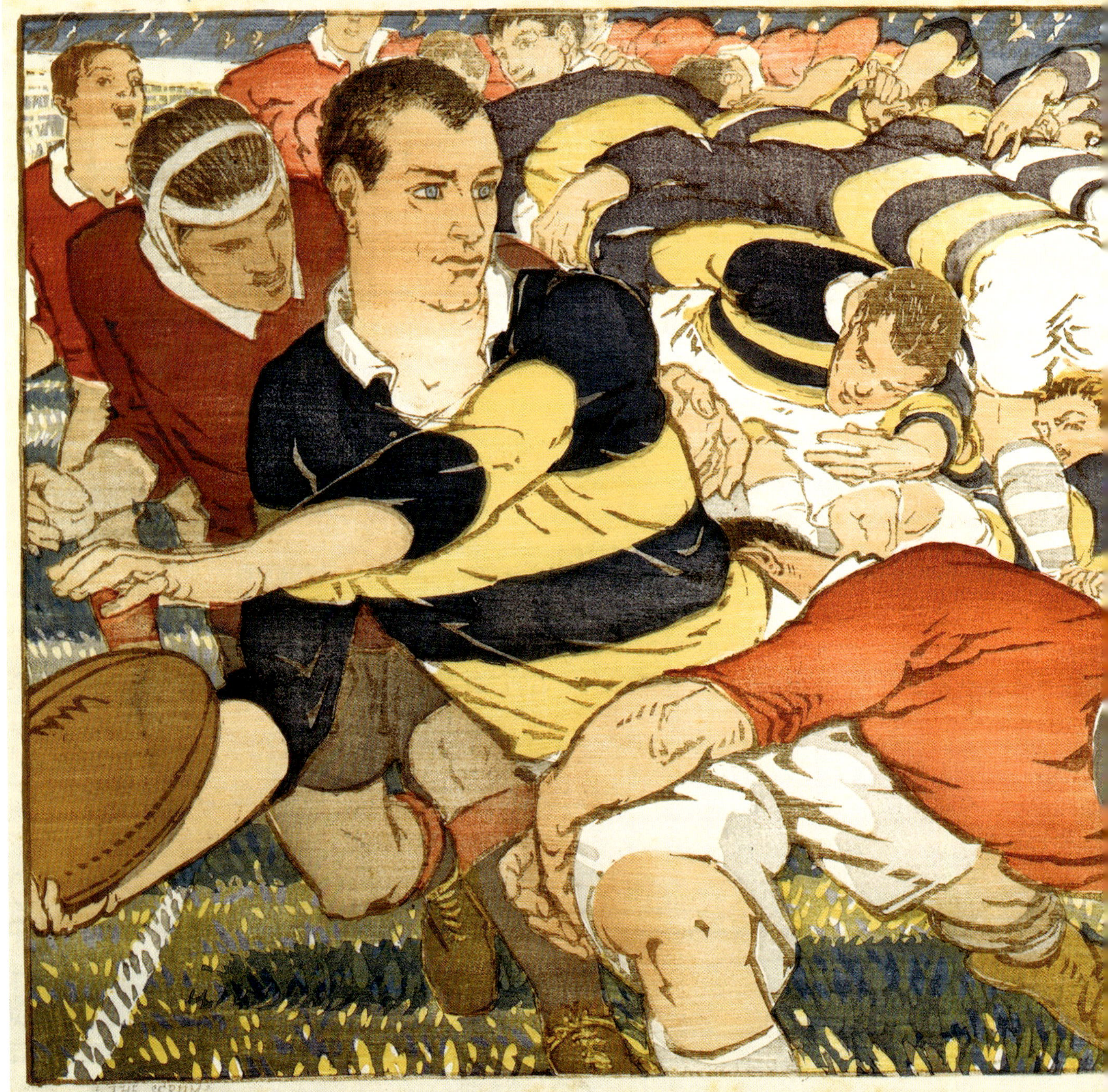
"THE SCRUM"

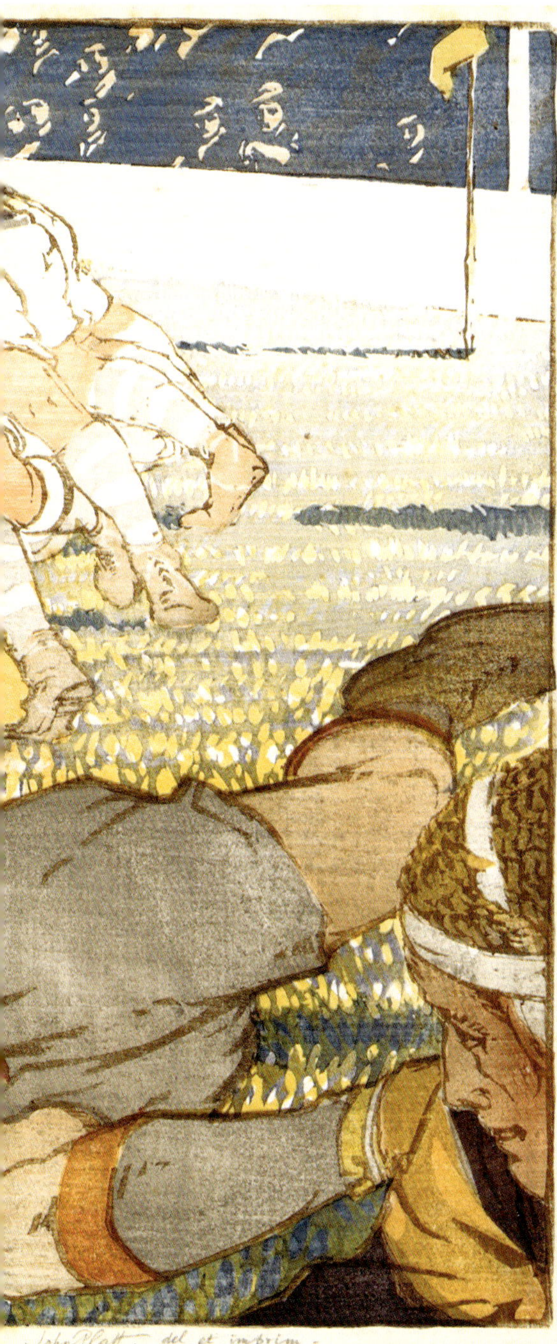

7 / *The Scrum*

1921 / 252 x 390 mm
private collection

Printed in eight colours on Japanese paper;
blue, brown, pink, purple, grey, yellow, sienna
with dark brown key block. Projected edition
of 100 (20 recorded, some impressions
numbered out of 50).

Exhibited: RA, 1922, no. 1108; SGPIC, 1922,
7th annual exhibition, no. 20.
Literature: *The Studio*, March 1922.
Collections: V&A, acquired 1986.
Posthumous edition: Edition of 75 prints
taken from the original key block for this
image in 2006. Printed on vellum by Simon
Lawrence of the Fleece Press, Huddersfield.

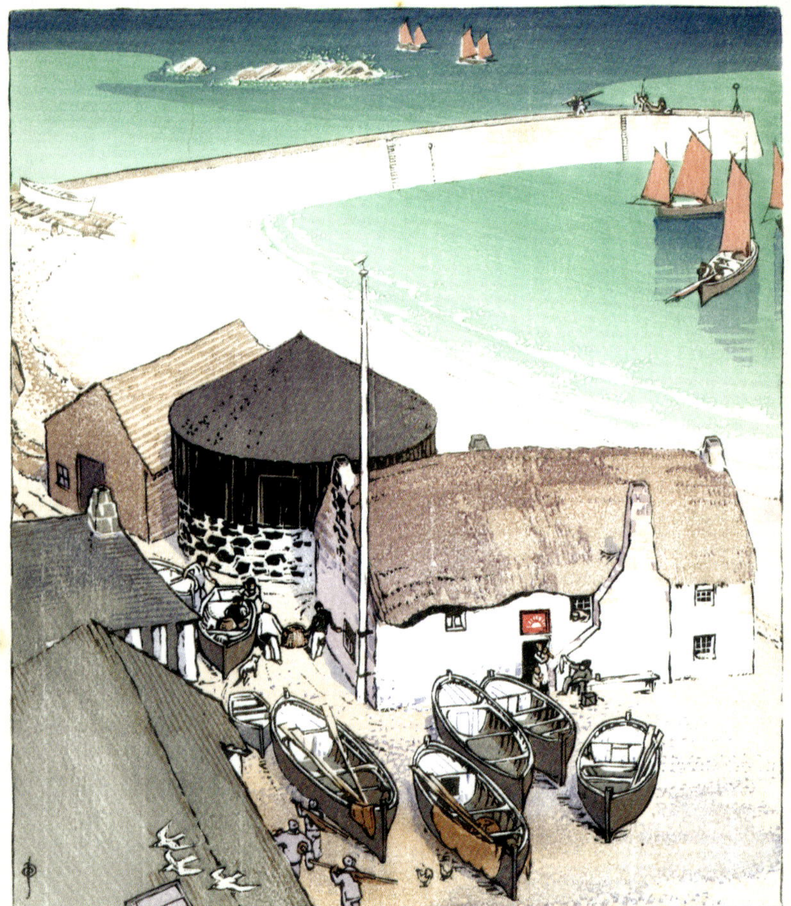

8 / *The Jetty, Sennen Cove*

December 1921 / 267 x 237 mm

Printed in seven colours on Japanese paper; green, grey, pink, brown, yellow, purple with black key block. Bears monogram lower left. Projected edition of 100 (126 recorded. Approximately another 26 above the edition printed after 1940 and numbered with the prefix E and D. Also, some numbered out of 150).

Exhibited: SGPIC, 1922, 7th annual exhibition, no. 6; Japan Society of London, Tokyo, 1925.
Literature: *The Studio*, April 1925; *Drawing and Design*, November 1924; *The Artist*, June 1934.
Collections: BM, presented by the Contemporary Art Society in 1924; V&A, acquired 1923; The Pushkin State Museum of Fine Arts, Moscow, gifted by Campbell Dodgson, Keeper of Prints and Drawings at the British Museum in 1926.

According to Platt's printing notes he chose a woodblock for this print where the wood grain would represent the water's edge.

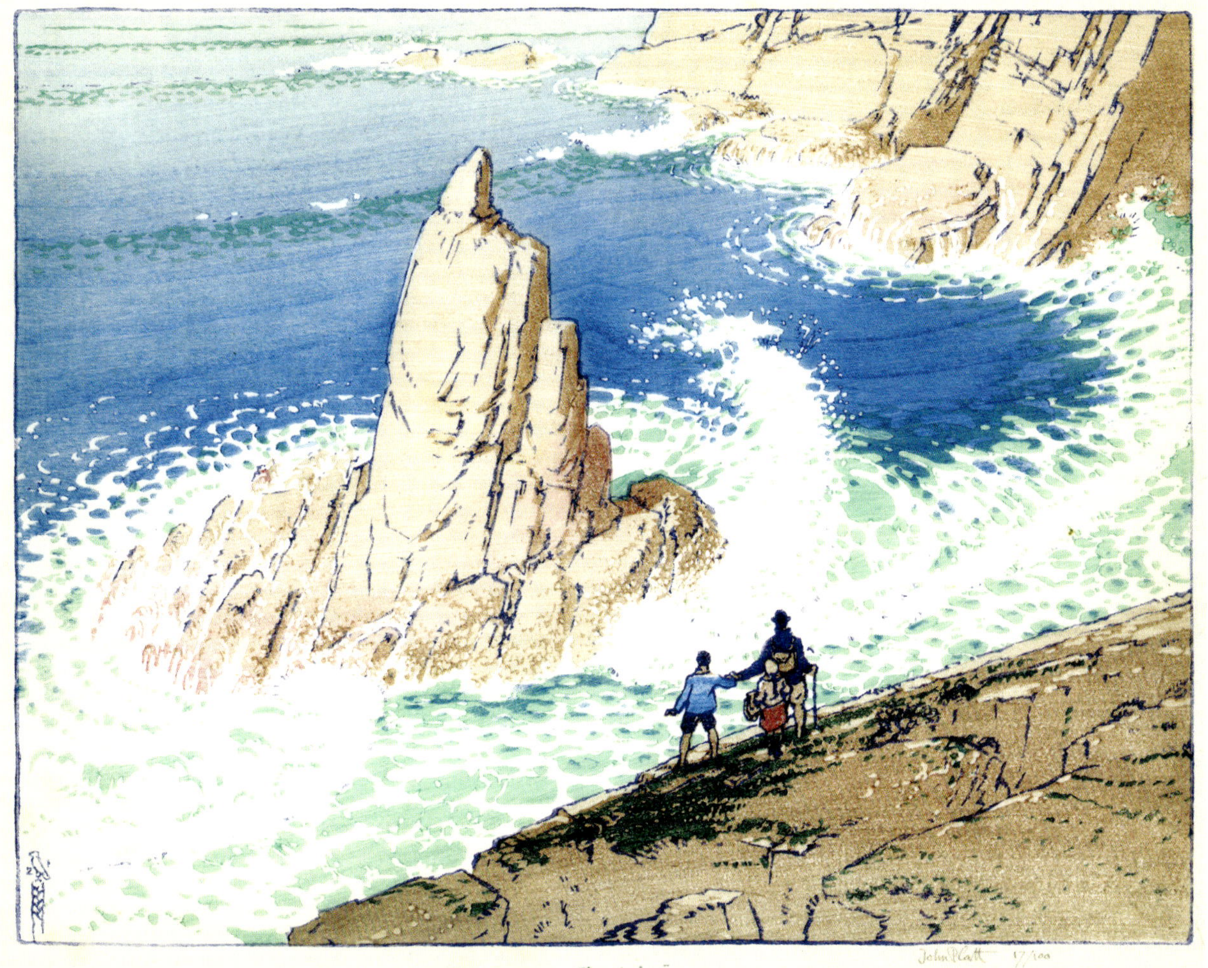

9 / *The Irish Lady, Land's End*

February 1922 / 202 x 265 mm

Printed in six colours on Japanese paper; blue, green, yellow, brown, red, purple with purple key block. Bears a seal in the block (lower left) of bird on a post and the date '21. Projected edition of 100 (78 recorded, some numbered out of 150).

Exhibited: SGPIC, 1922, 7th annual exhibition, no. 13; SGPIC, 1923, 8th annual exhibition, no. 18.
Literature: *The Studio*, November 1925; *Drawing and Design*, November 1924.
Collections: V&A, acquired 1923.

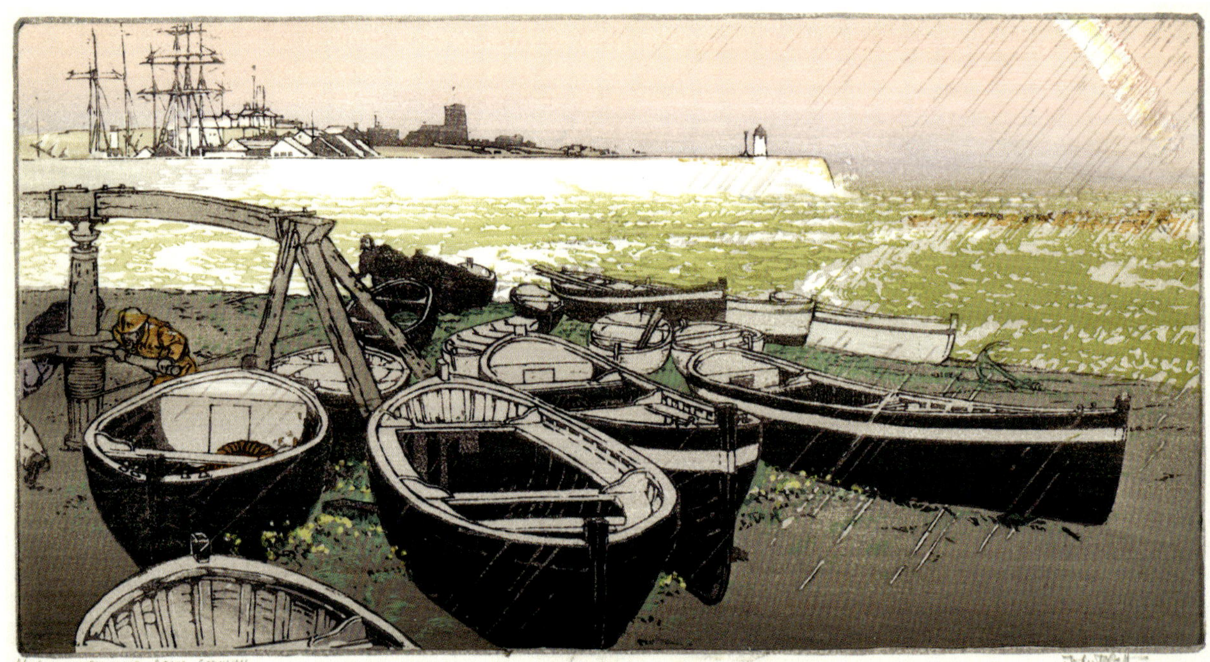

10 / *Pilchard Boats, Cornwall*

November 1922 / 166 x 320 mm

Printed in six colours on Japanese paper; dark green, light green, grey, pink, orange with dark grey key block. Projected edition of 100 (78 recorded).

Exhibited: SGPIC, 1923, 8th annual exhibition, no. 11.
Literature: *The Artist*, May 1934.
Collections: BM, presented by the Contemporary Art Society in 1926; V&A, acquired 1923.

11 / *Entering the Port, St. Tropez*

March 1923 / 328 x 229 mm

Printed in seven colours on Japanese paper;
orange, yellow, buff, grey, pink, purple, blue
with grey key block. Projected edition of 100
(150 recorded, a further 50 prints above the
edition numbered in Roman numerals).

Exhibited: SGPIC, 1924, 9th annual
exhibition, no. 41.
Literature: *The Studio*, November 1925;
Drawing and Design, November 1924.
Collections: BM, presented by the
Contemporary Art Society in 1932; V&A,
acquired 1923; Ulster Museum, Belfast,
acquired 1931; Gallery Oldham, acquired 1926.

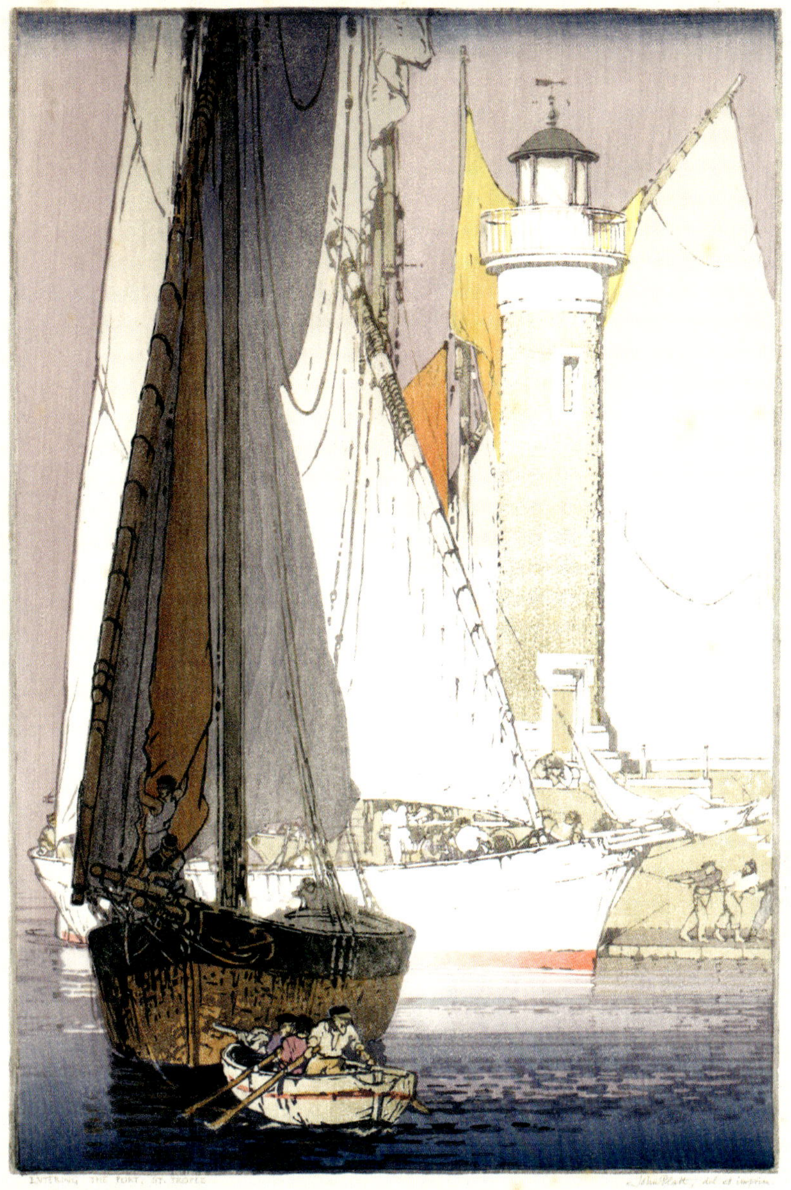

1924 / 342 x 262 mm

Printed in three colours on Japanese paper; sepia, grey with black key block. Projected edition of 100 (120 recorded, 20 prints above the edition numbered with Roman numerals).

Exhibited: Los Angeles Museum, Los Angeles, 1925, 7th International Printmakers Exhibition (organised by the Printmakers Society of California), winner of the 'Storrow Prize'; SGPIC, 1925, 10th annual exhibition, no. 52; RA, 1940, no. 995.
Literature: *The Studio*, November 1925; *The Artist*, March 1934.
Collections: BM, presented by the Contemporary Art Society, 1927; V&A, acquired 1925; New Walk Museum & Art Gallery, Leicester, acquired 1925; Whitworth Art Gallery, acquired 1933; Ipswich Art Gallery, acquired 1928. The drawing for this print was acquired by the Tate (Duveen Bequest 1924, acquisition number: 3875).

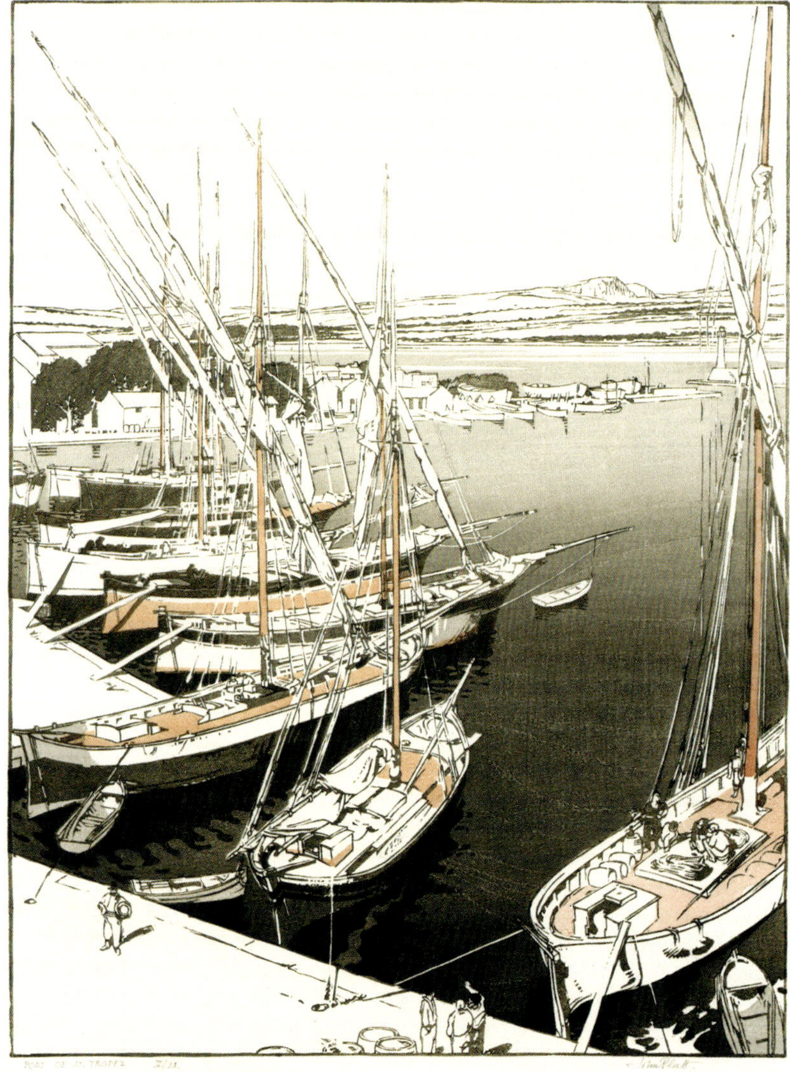

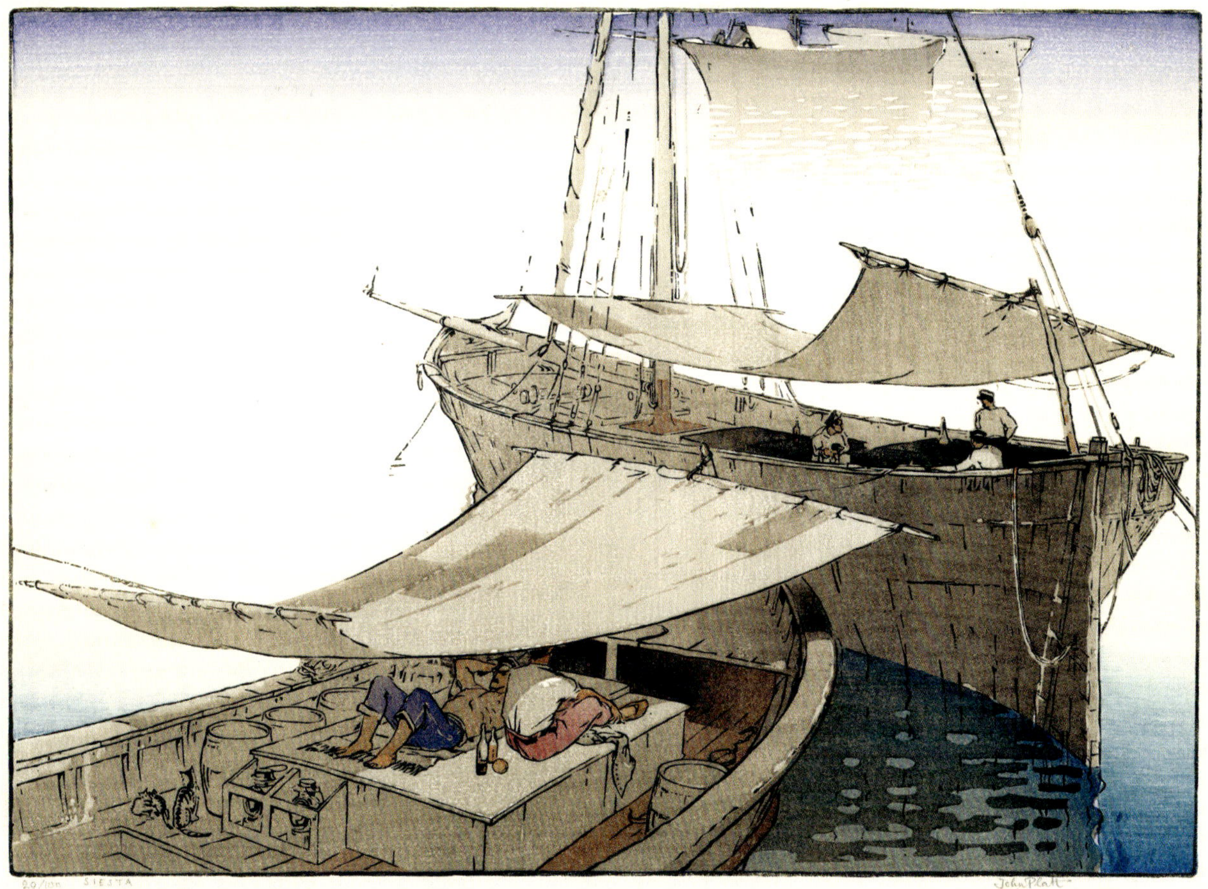

13 / *Siesta*

December 1925 / 230 x 330 mm

Printed in six colours on Japanese paper; pink, blue, brown, purple, grey with black key block. Projected edition of 100 (100 recorded, plus three trial proofs).

Exhibited: SGPIC, 1926, 11th annual exhibition, no. 9.
Literature: *The Artist*, April 1934.
Collections: BM, presented by the Contemporary Art Society in 1928; V&A, acquired 1926; New Walk Museum & Art Gallery, Leicester, acquired 1927; Hereford Museum and Art Gallery, acquired 1929.

14 / *Red Chestnut no. 1*

February 1927 / 384 x 220 mm

Printed in eight colours on Japanese paper;
light blue, dark blue, light green, dark green,
pink, purple, orange, black with partial
key block in black. Projected edition of 68
(68 recorded: nos. 59–60, second scheme,
experimental proofs 1–2; numbers 61–67,
advanced proofs 1–7; number 68, trial of
third scheme).

Collections: V&A, acquired 1986.

Including a blue border on three sides only.

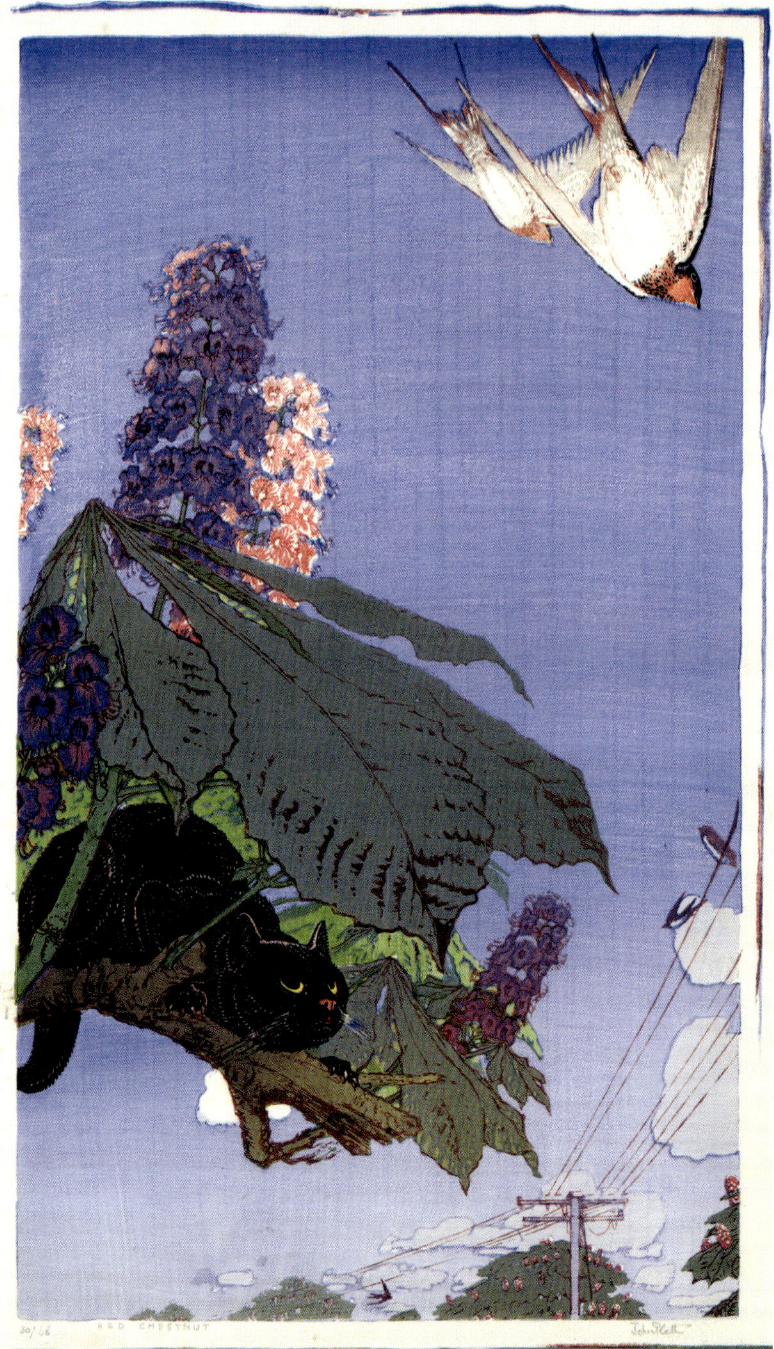

15 / *Red Chestnut no. 2*

December 1927 / 384 x 220 mm

Printed in eight colours on Japanese paper;
light blue, dark blue, light green, dark green,
pink, purple, orange, black with partial key
block in black. Projected edition of 150
(19 recorded).

Exhibited: SGPIC, 1927, 12th annual
exhibition, no. 21.
Literature: *The Artist*, July 1934.
Collections: V&A, acquired 1986.

A variation of cat. 14 with no blue background
and with the telegraph wires, trees and some
swallows removed. Some impressions with
the artist's device in the block (lower right).
Includes a black border on all four sides.

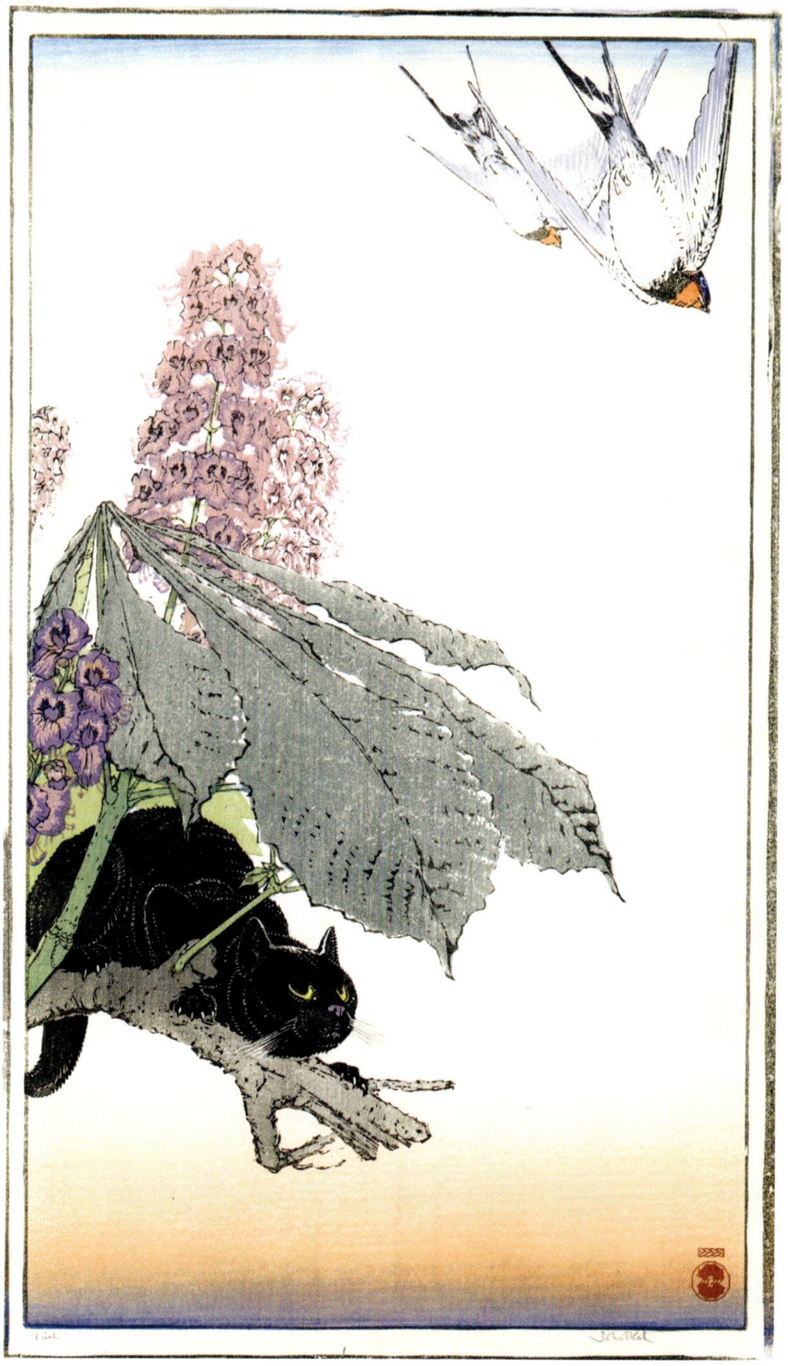

16 / *Brixham Town*

October 1927 / 254 x 355 mm

Printed in seven colours on Japanese paper;
blue, grey, purple, pink, green, brown with
black partial key block. Projected edition
of 150 (150 recorded).

Exhibited: SGPIC, 1928, 13th annual
exhibition, no. 2; SGPIC, 1947, no. 57.
Literature: *The Artist*, May 1934.
Collections: BM, presented by the
Contemporary Art Society in 1932; V&A,
acquired 1931.

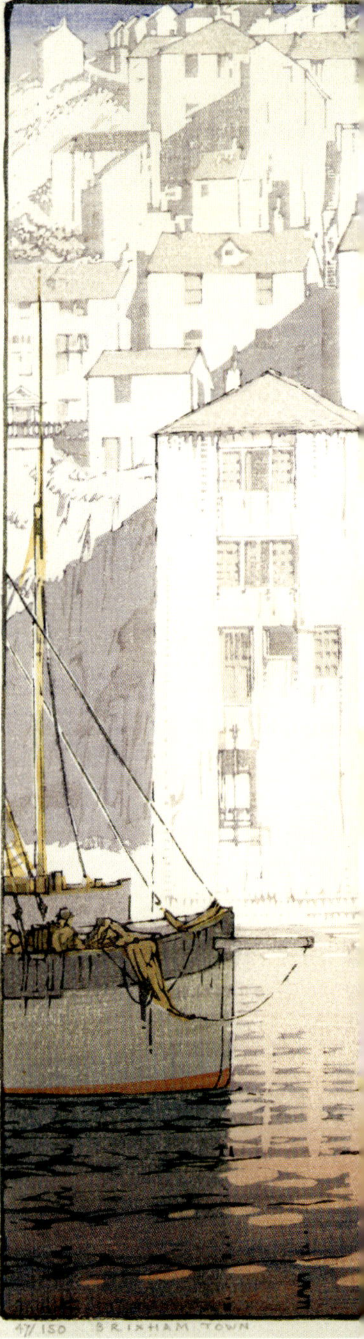

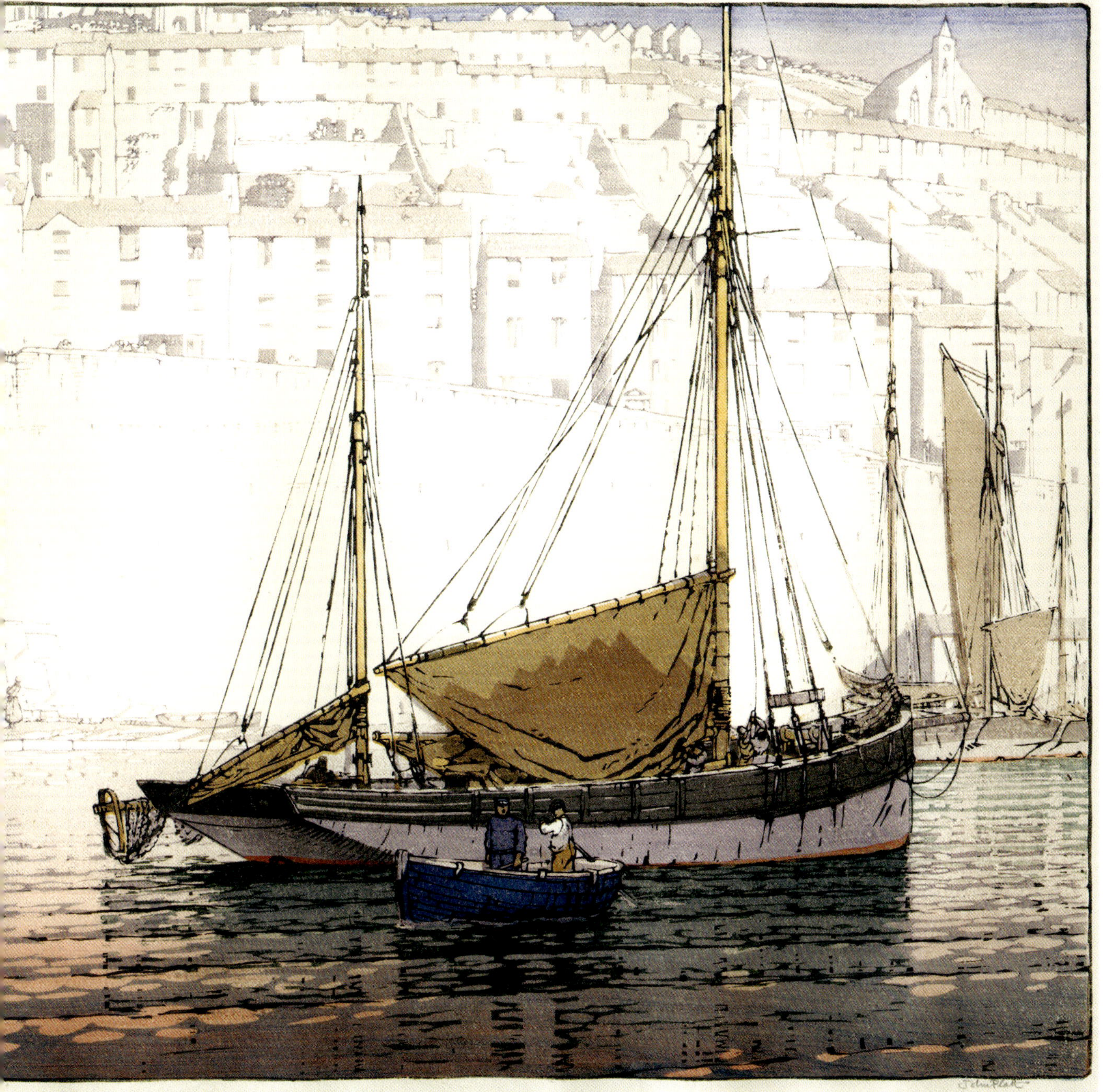

17 / *Staithes, Yorkshire*

December 1927 / 330 x 260 mm

Printed in six colours on Japanese paper;
blue, brown, green, yellow, light red, grey
with grey partial key block. Projected edition
of 150 (122 recorded).

Exhibited: SGPIC, 1928, 13th annual
exhibition, no. 1.
Literature: *The Artist*, September 1934.
Collections: Manchester Art Gallery,
acquired 1944.

Platt recorded in his printing notes that it
took 14 days to cut the blocks for this print.

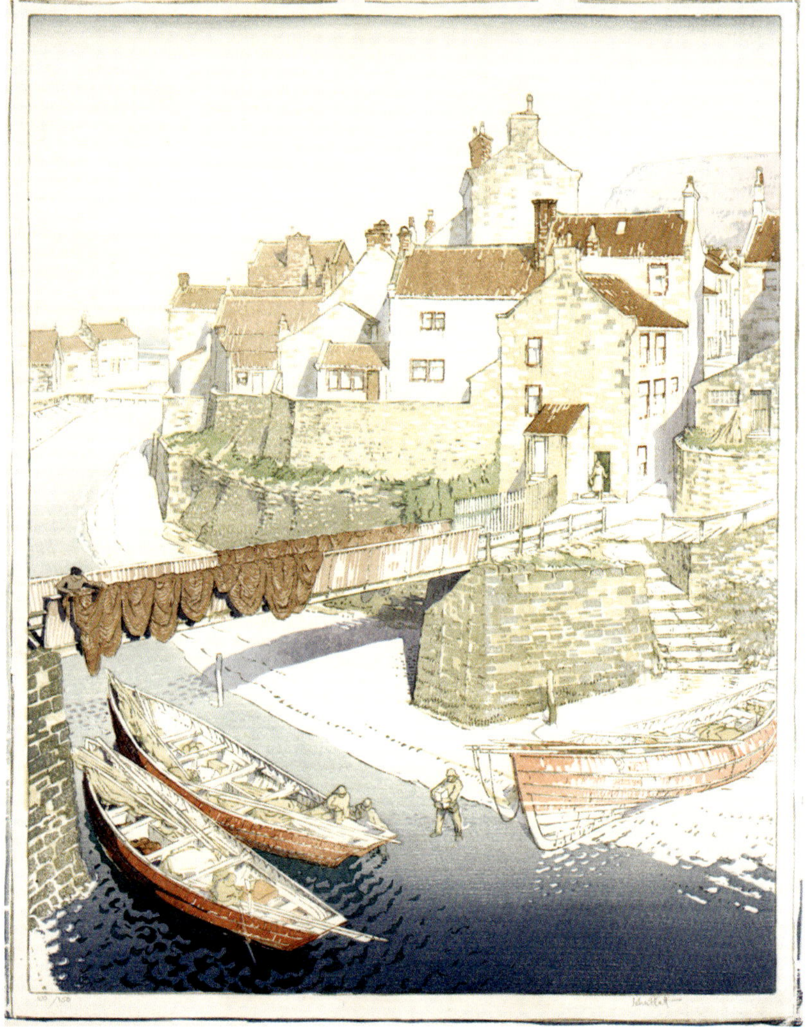

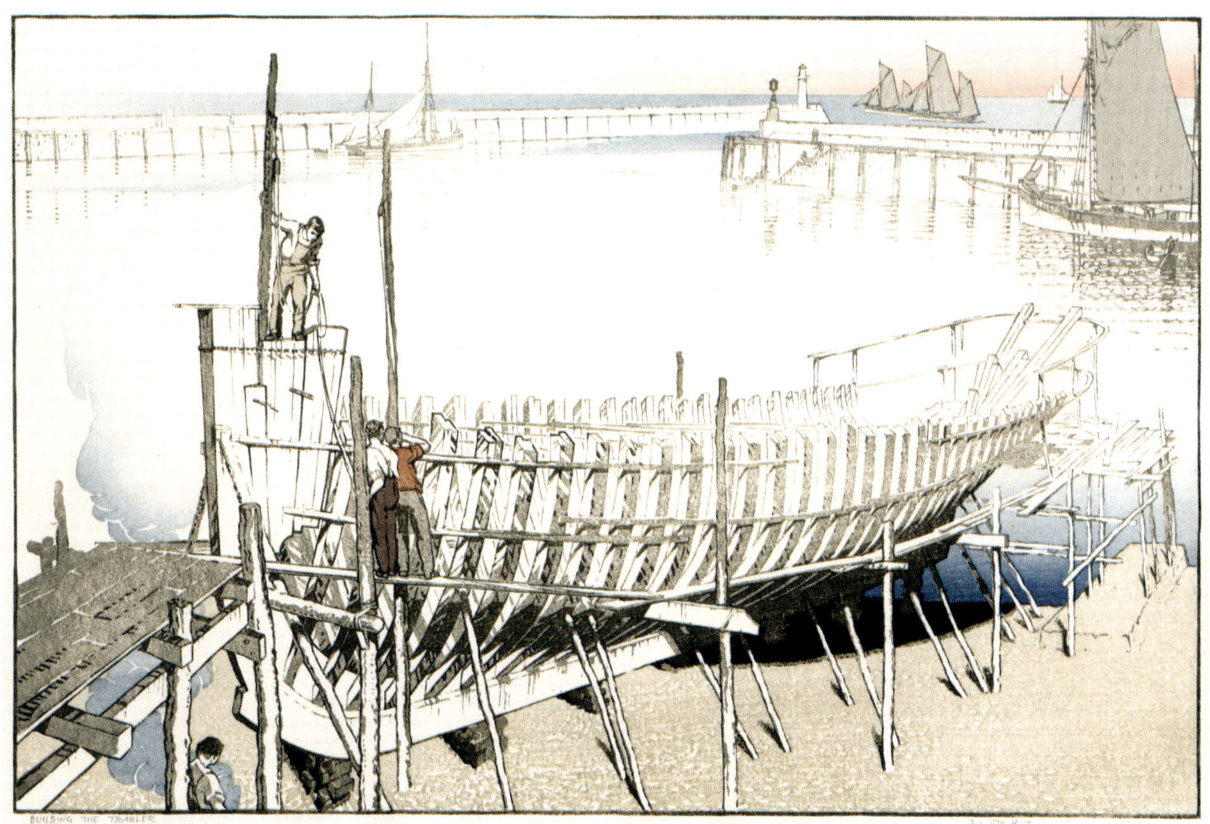

18 / *Building the Trawler*

March 1929 / 230 x 355 mm

Printed in five colours on Japanese paper;
blue, grey, pink, brown with black partial key
block. Projected edition of 150 (72 recorded,
including 8 trial proofs marked a–h).

Exhibited: RA, 1929, no. 747; SGPIC, 1930,
15th annual exhibition, no. 63; NEAC, 1928,
no. 329.
Literature: *The Artist*, April 1934.
Collections: V&A, acquired 1931.

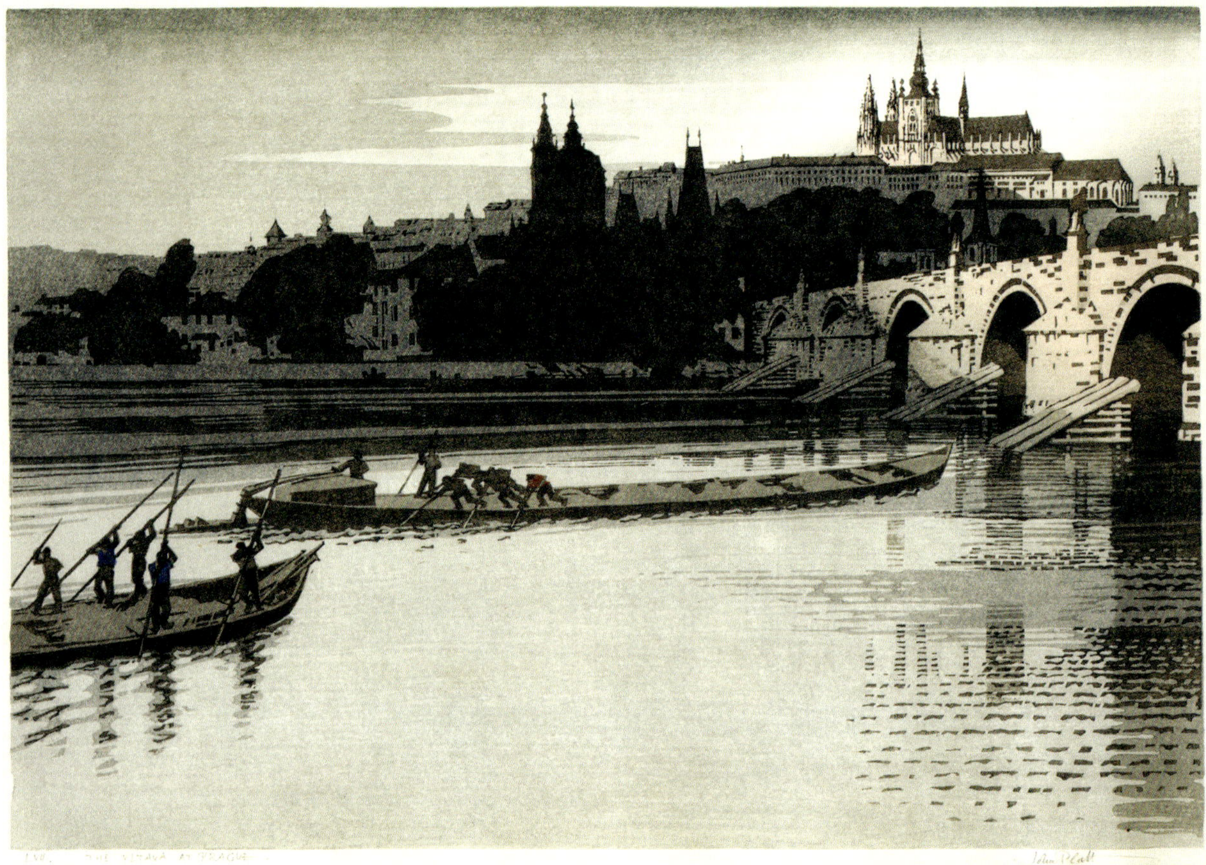

19 / *The Vltava at Prague*

May 1930 / 245 x 360 mm

Printed in five colours on Japanese paper; blue, pink, grey, dark grey, brown, no key block. Also printed in grey and black only. Projected edition of 150 (64 recorded).

Exhibited: RA, 1939, no. 770; SGPIC, 1947, no. 55; NEAC, 1928, no. 329.
Literature: *The Artist*, March 1934.
Collections: Whitworth Art Gallery, acquired 1945; The Atkinson, Southport, acquired 1932.

Platt visited Prague in 1928 as Principal of Leicester College of Art to attend the International Congress of Art and Industrial Design.

20 / *Mullion Cove*

January 1931 / 230 x 258 mm

Printed in seven colours on Japanese paper;
grey, black, green, blue, brown, light red with
partial key block in black. Projected edition
of 150 (80 recorded).

Exhibited: RA, 1931, no. 1006; SGPIC, 1931,
16th annual exhibition, no. 4; 1934, 19th
annual exhibition, no. 66; SGPIC, 1947,
no. 56.
Collections: BM, presented by the
Contemporary Art Society in 1934; V&A,
acquired 1986; Doncaster Art Gallery,
acquired 1943.

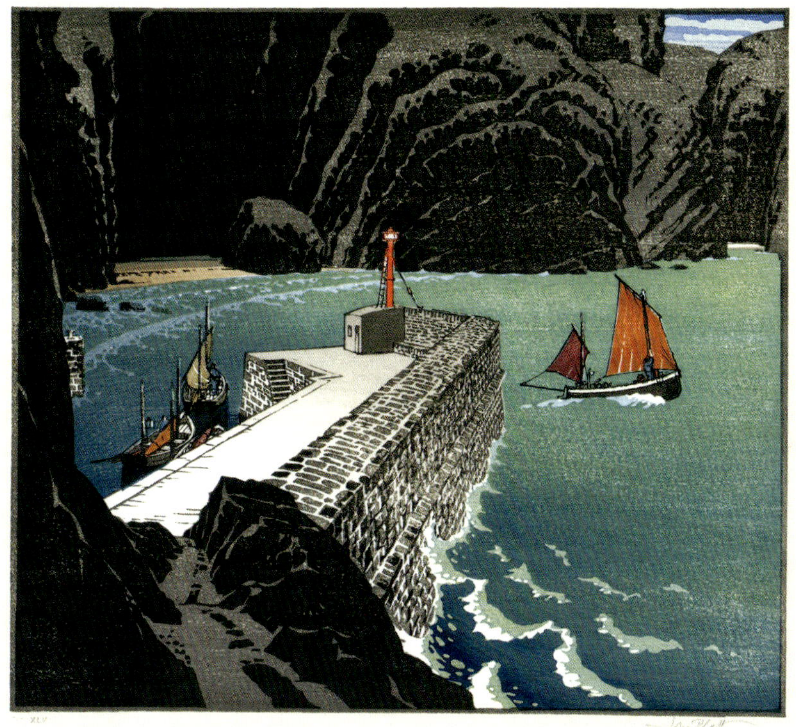

21 / *The Echoing Shore*

October 1931 / 292 x 240 mm

Printed in eight/nine colours on Japanese
paper in three different colour versions:
i. with red scarf and green background;
black, blue, yellow, red, light green, dark
green, light grey with key block in red (body)
and black (drapery); **ii.** with blue scarf and
green background; light grey, dark grey,
purple, blue, dark blue, light green, brown
and key block in red (body) and brown
(drapery); **iii.** with blue scarf and blue
background; black, purple, red, pink, blue,
dark blue, green, grey, dark grey with key
block in red (body) and purple (drapery).
No projected edition (recorded: i. 17; ii. 1;
iii. 5).

Exhibited: SGPIC, 1933, 18th annual
exhibition, no. 87; SGPIC, 1934, 19th annual
exhibition, no. 22.
Literature: *The Studio*, January 1933;
The Artist, July 1934.
Collections: BM, presented by the
Contemporary Art Society in 1934.

Platt produced a watercolour on silk of the
same design (private collection).

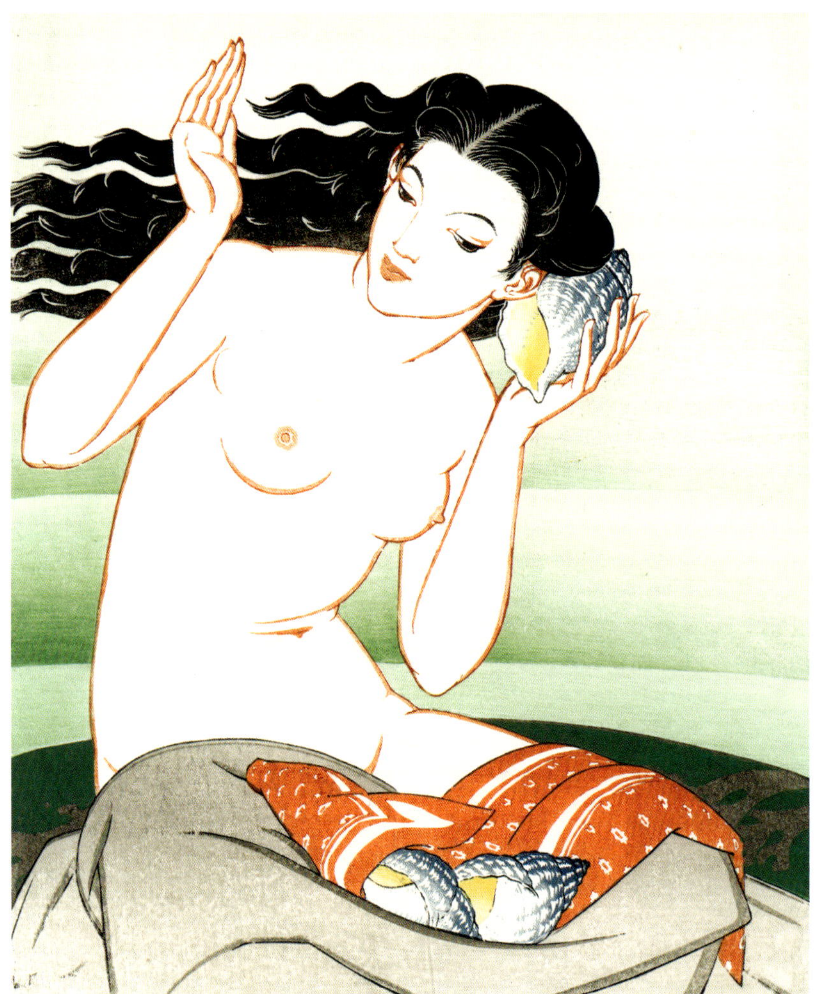

22 / *Red Bull*

March 1932 / 212 x 274 mm

Printed in seven colours on Japanese paper;
dark grey, light grey, yellow, dark green, light
green, dark brown, light brown, no key block.
No projected edition (9 recorded).

Exhibited: RA, 1933, no. 979; SGPIC, 1933,
18th annual exhibition, no. 30; SGPIC, 1935,
20th annual exhibition, no. 8; SGPIC, 1937,
22nd annual exhibition, no. 63.
Literature: *The Artist*, August 1934.
Collections: BM, presented by the
Contemporary Art Society in 1941.

In Platt's book *Colour Woodcuts* he illustrates
the four states for *Red Bull* (see p. 23 herein).
Another trial print also exists with the bull,
a blue sky and a geometric green background.

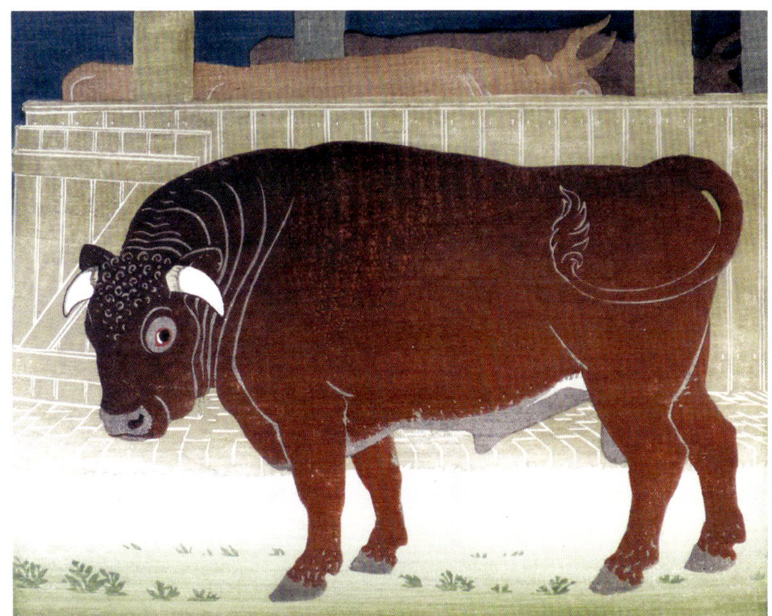

23 / *The Bull Across the Path*

1932 / 245 x 274 mm

Printed in eight colours on Japanese paper;
dark grey, light grey, yellow, blue, dark brown,
light brown, green, light green, no key block.
No projected edition (4 recorded).

Exhibited: RA, 1939, no. 768.

A variation of cat. 22 with a replacement
block for the interior of the shippen (cow-
pen) showing back view of three cows and
a cowman, and two extra grass blocks in
the foreground.

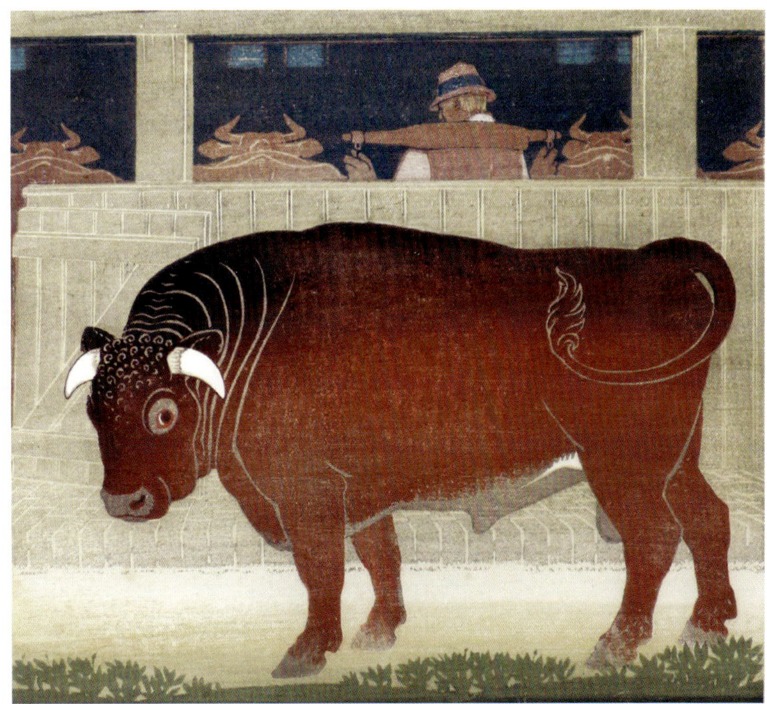

24 / *Sails*

1933 / 350 x 247 mm

Printed in seven colours on Japanese paper;
blue, green, pink, brown, black, light grey,
dark grey, no key block. Two alternative
colour backgrounds were printed: blue and
green. No projected edition (32 recorded).

Exhibited: RA, 1934, no. 842.; SGPIC, 1934,
19th annual exhibition, no. 61.
Literature: *The Artist*, September 1934.

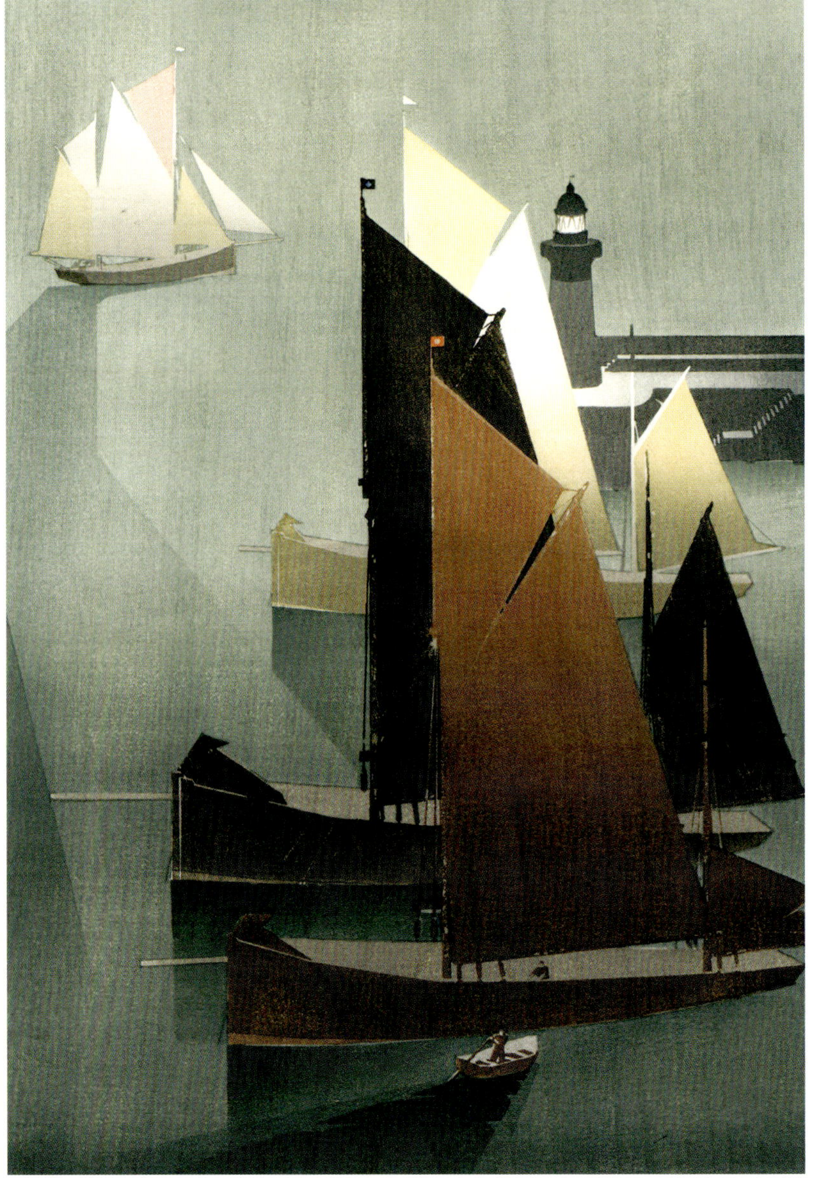

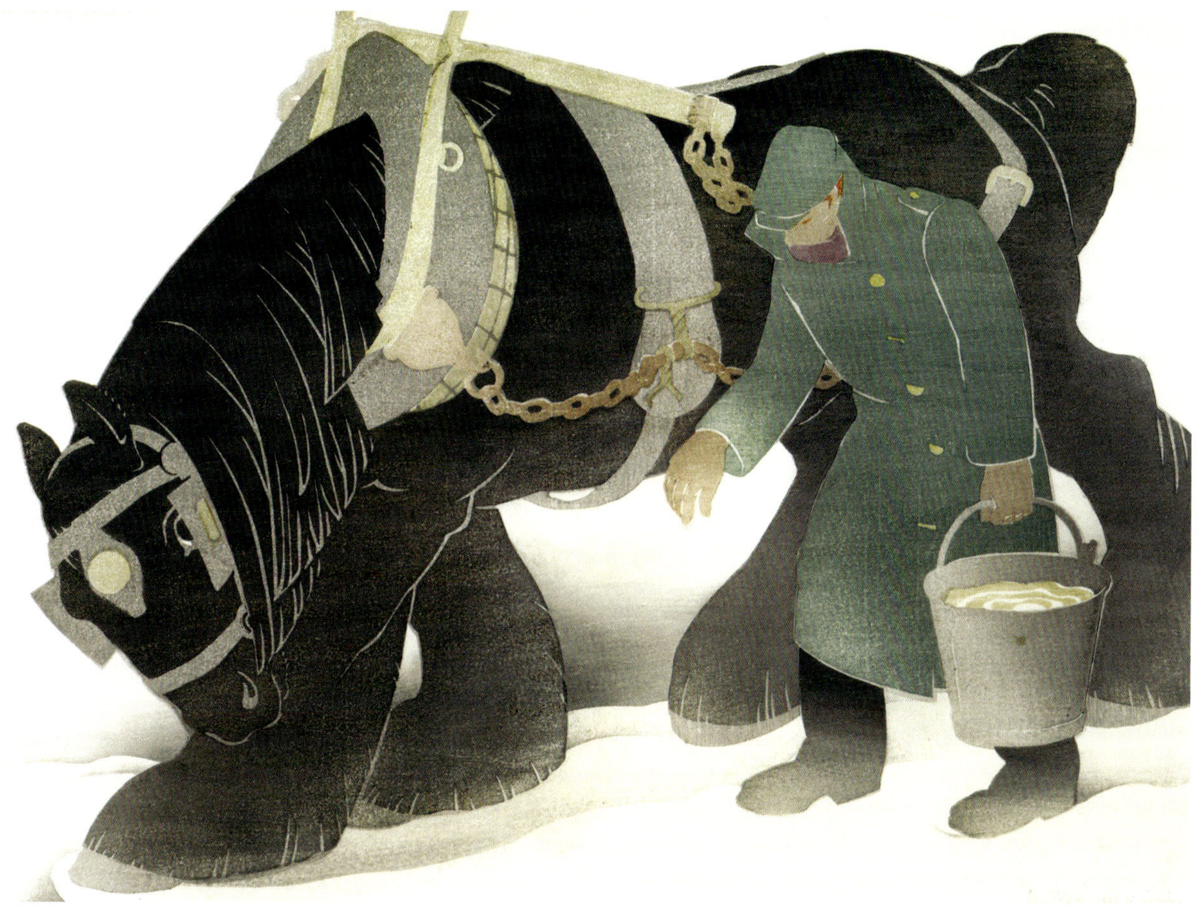

25 / *Horse*

October 1934 / 267 x 368 mm

Printed in six colours on Japanese paper;
black, grey, green, yellow, red, brown, no key
block. Three separate printings recorded by
Platt in the printing notes. **i.** 1934 printed
with 'snowflakes' cut into block. **ii.** 1946
printed with skyblock filled to remove
snowflakes. **iii.** 1948 with new skyblock recut
without snowflakes. No projected editions
(recorded: i, 10, plus a trial proof touched
with white and a sky printed on a separate
block and superimposed; ii. 14; iii. 8).

Exhibited: RA, 1935, no. 1125; NEAC, 1934,
no. 137; SGPIC, 1935, 20th annual exhibition,
no. 6; SGPIC, 1947, no. 51.
Collections: V&A, acquired 1986.

Platt records in his printing notes that the
second printing of 14 prints took one week.

26 / *Lamb*

October 1934 / 190 x 210 mm

Printed in five colours on Japanese paper; purple, black, grey, green, yellow, no key block. No projected edition (28 recorded).

Exhibited: RA, 1935, no. 1175; SGPIC, 1935, 20th annual exhibition, no. 5; SGPIC, 1947, no. 53; NEAC, 1934, no. 137.
Literature: *The Artist*, January 1937.
Collections: New Walk Museum & Art Gallery, Leicester, transferred from School Loans Service, 1977.

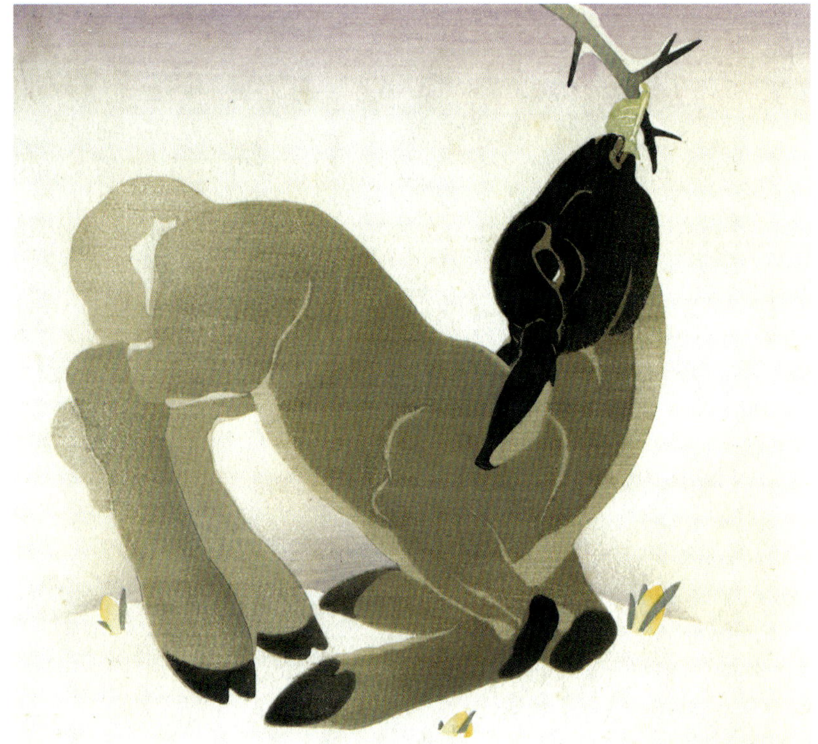

27 / *Two Monkeys (Macaques)*

March 1935 / 273 x 203 mm*

Printed in five colours on Japanese paper;
light brown, dark brown, light grey, dark
grey, beige, no key block. No projected
edition (35 recorded).

Exhibited: RA, no. 1057; SGPIC, 1935, 20th
annual exhibition, no. 7; SGPIC, 1947, no. 52;
NEAC, 1935, no. 313.
Literature: *The Artist*, January 1937.
Collections: BM, presented by the
Contemporary Art Society in 1936; New
Walk Museum & Art Gallery, Leicester,
purchased by Leicester Society of Artists in
1936 (also, another working proof transferred
from Schools Loan Service, 1977); Whitworth
Art Gallery, transferred from the University
of Manchester; History of Art Department
in 1960.

Platt made sketches of macaques at the
London Zoological Gardens in Regents Park
for this design.

*Artist designated size 380 x 205 mm

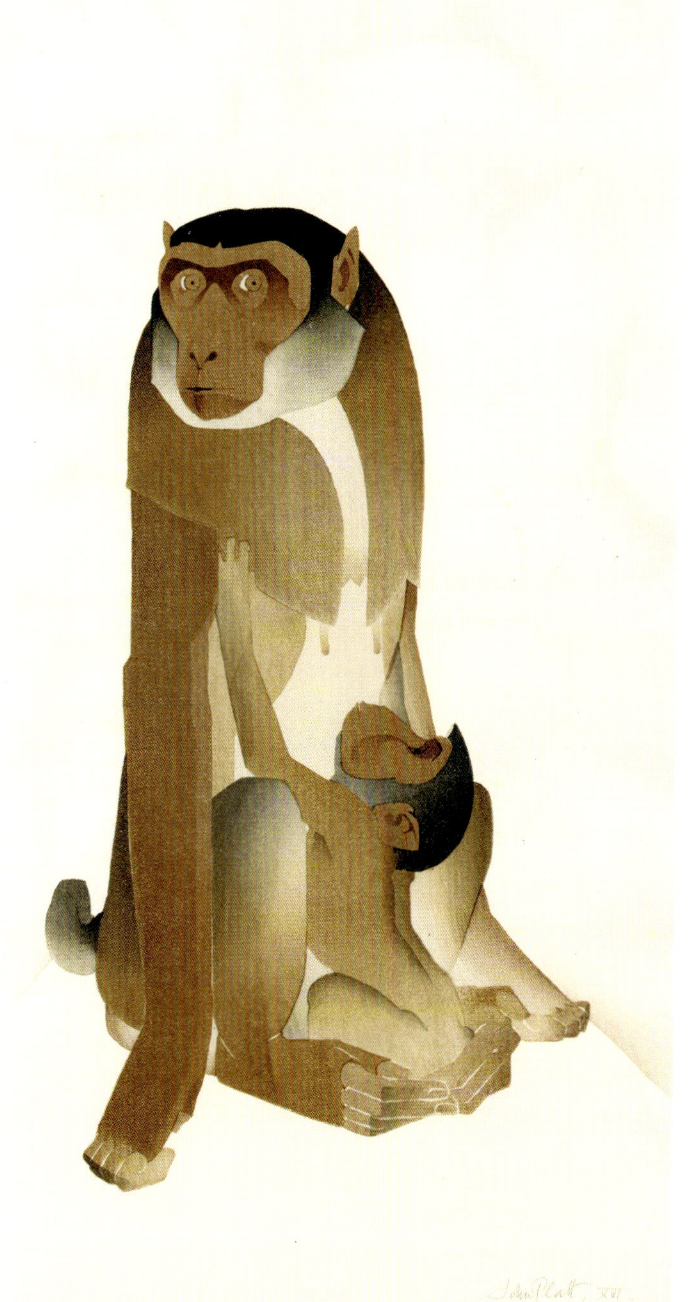

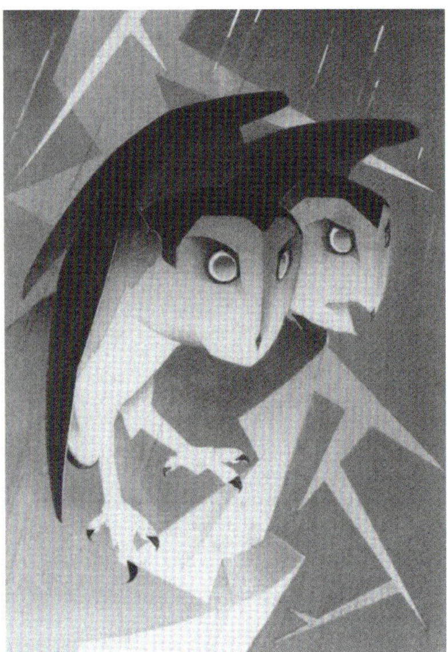

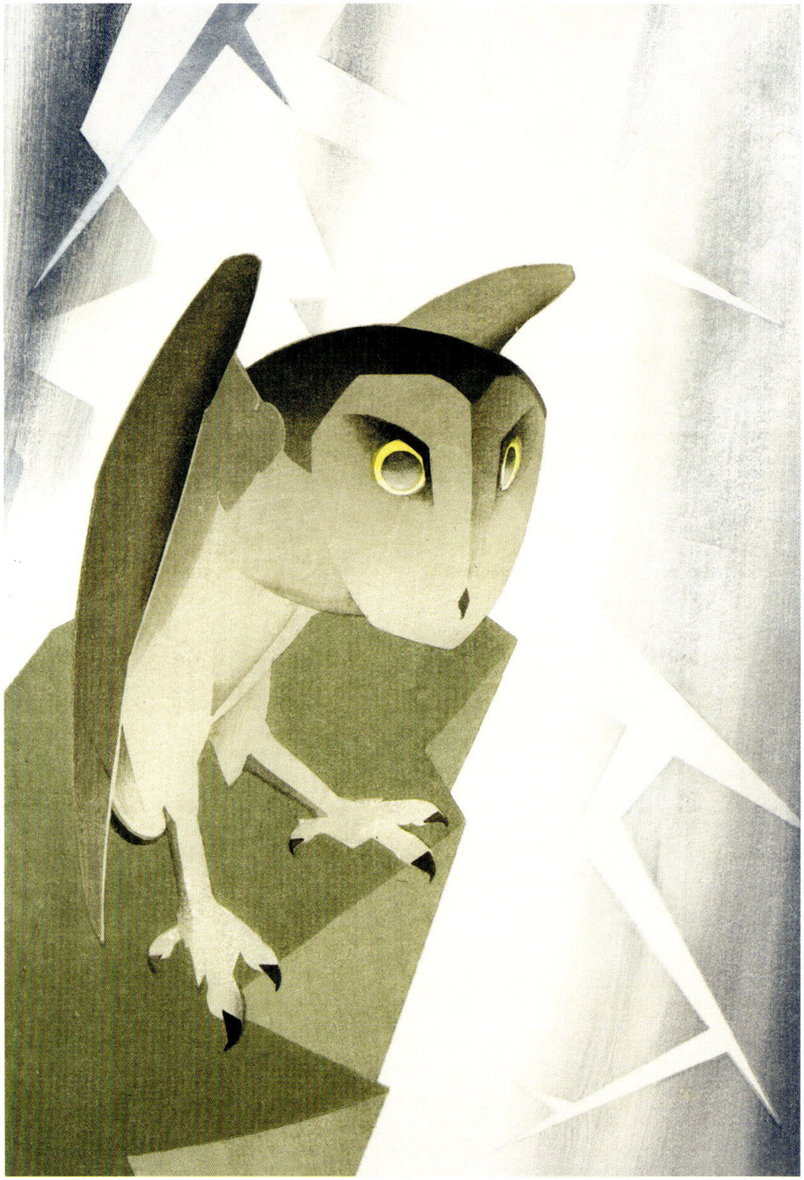

28 / *Birds of Fear*

August 1935 / 320 x 227 mm

Printed in seven colours on Japanese paper; blue, pink, black, light grey, dark grey, light brown, dark brown, no key block. No projected edition. Only two trial prints made.

29 / *Bird of Fear*

November 1935 / 322 x 190 mm

Printed in seven colours on Japanese paper; blue, yellow, dark grey, light grey, dark green, light green, black, no key block. No projected edition (5 recorded).

Exhibited: SGPIC, 1935, 20th annual exhibition, no. 9.
Literature: *The Artist*, January 1937.

30 / *Flame*

March 1936 / 365 x 233 mm

Printed in ten colours on Japanese paper;
dark blue, light blue, dark grey, light grey,
dark red, yellow, crimson, dark brown, light
brown, turquoise, no key block. No projected
edition (19 recorded).

Exhibited: SGPIC, 1936, 21st annual
exhibition, no. 7.
Collections: BM, presented by
Contemporary Art Society in 1937.

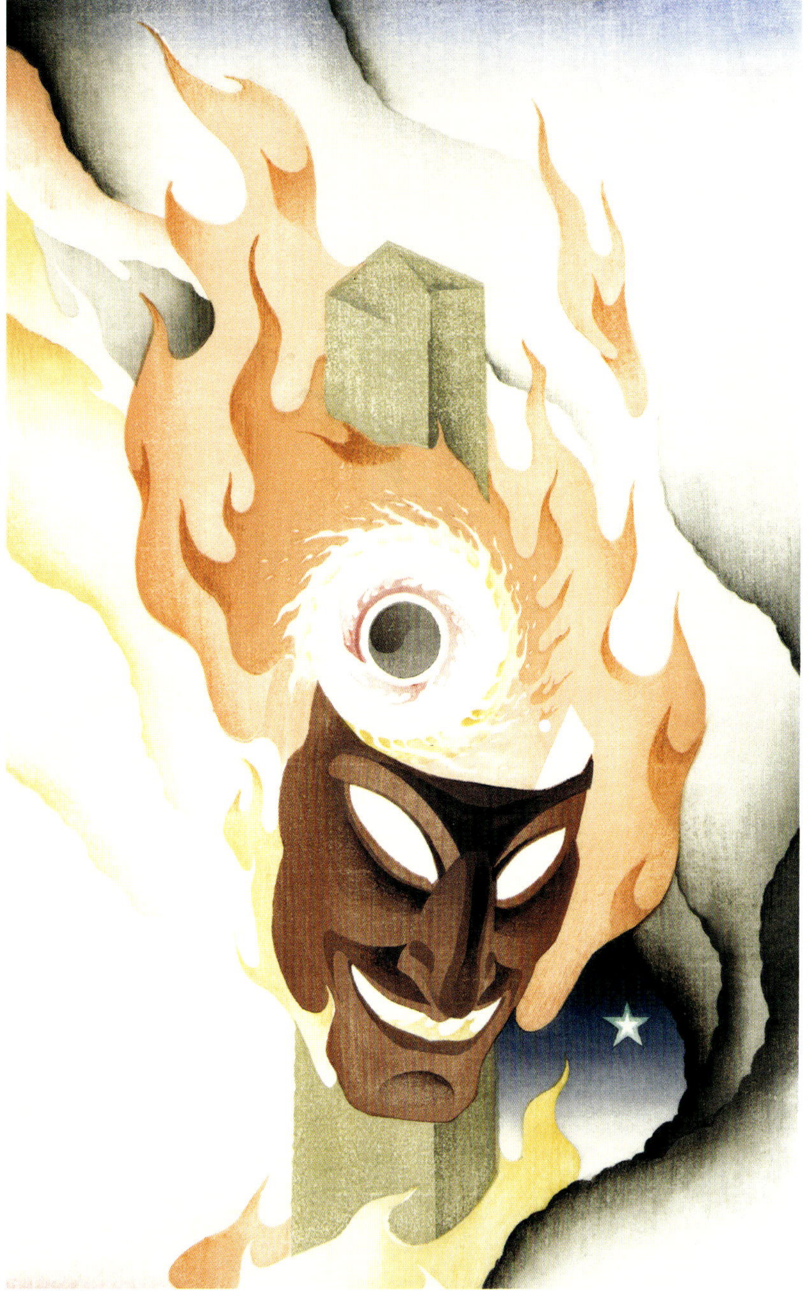

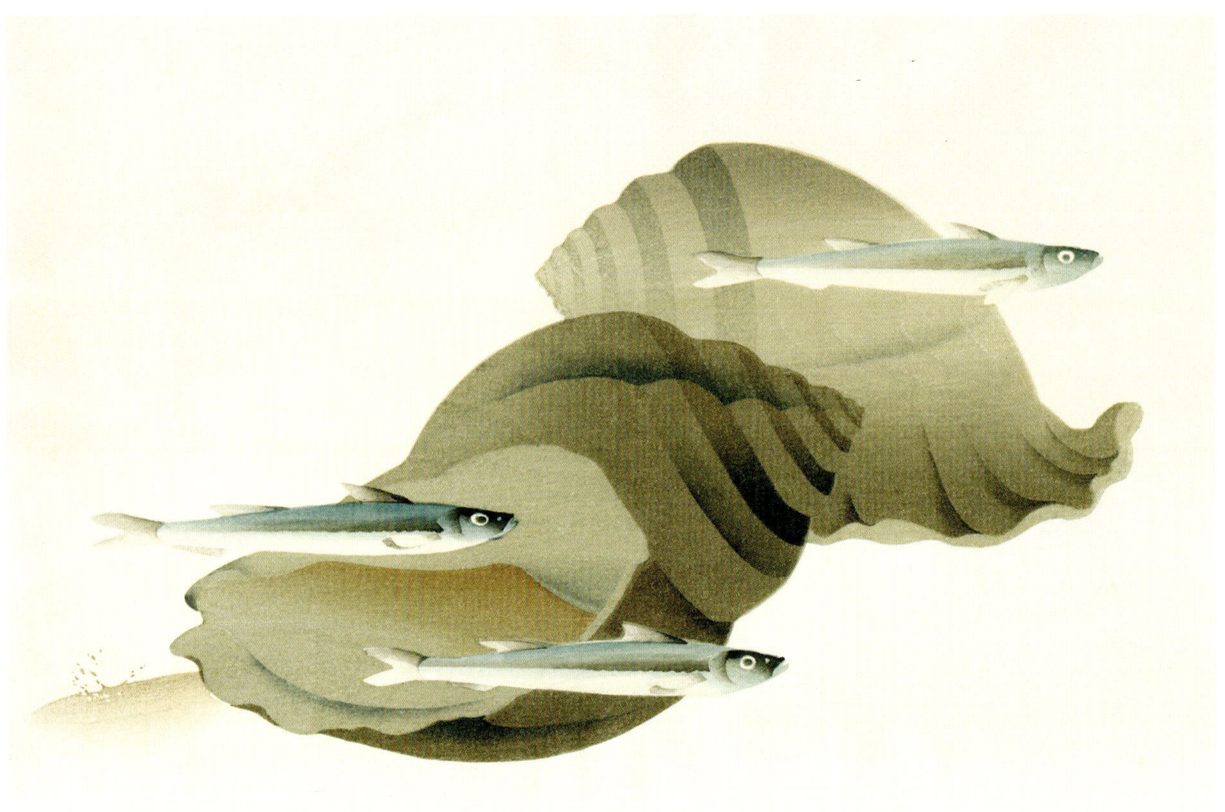

31 / *Two Shells*

March 1936 / 185 x 345 mm*

Printed in four colours on Japanese paper;
turquoise, light grey, dark grey, light brown,
no key block. No projected edition
(29 recorded).

Exhibited: RA, 1936, no. 1244; SGPIC, 1936,
21st annual exhibition, no. 44; SGPIC, 1947,
no. 54.

*Artist designated size 234 x 374 mm

32 / *Lapwings*

October 1936 / 415 x 205 mm

Printed in seven colours on Japanese paper;
light grey, dark grey, blue/grey, light brown,
dark brown, pink, black, no key block. No
projected edition (22 recorded).

Exhibited: RA, 1938, no. 1084; SGPIC, 1936,
21st annual exhibition, no. 8; NEAC, 1936,
no. 333.
Literature: *The Artist*, January 1937.
Collections: V&A, presented by the
Contemporary Art Society in 1937.

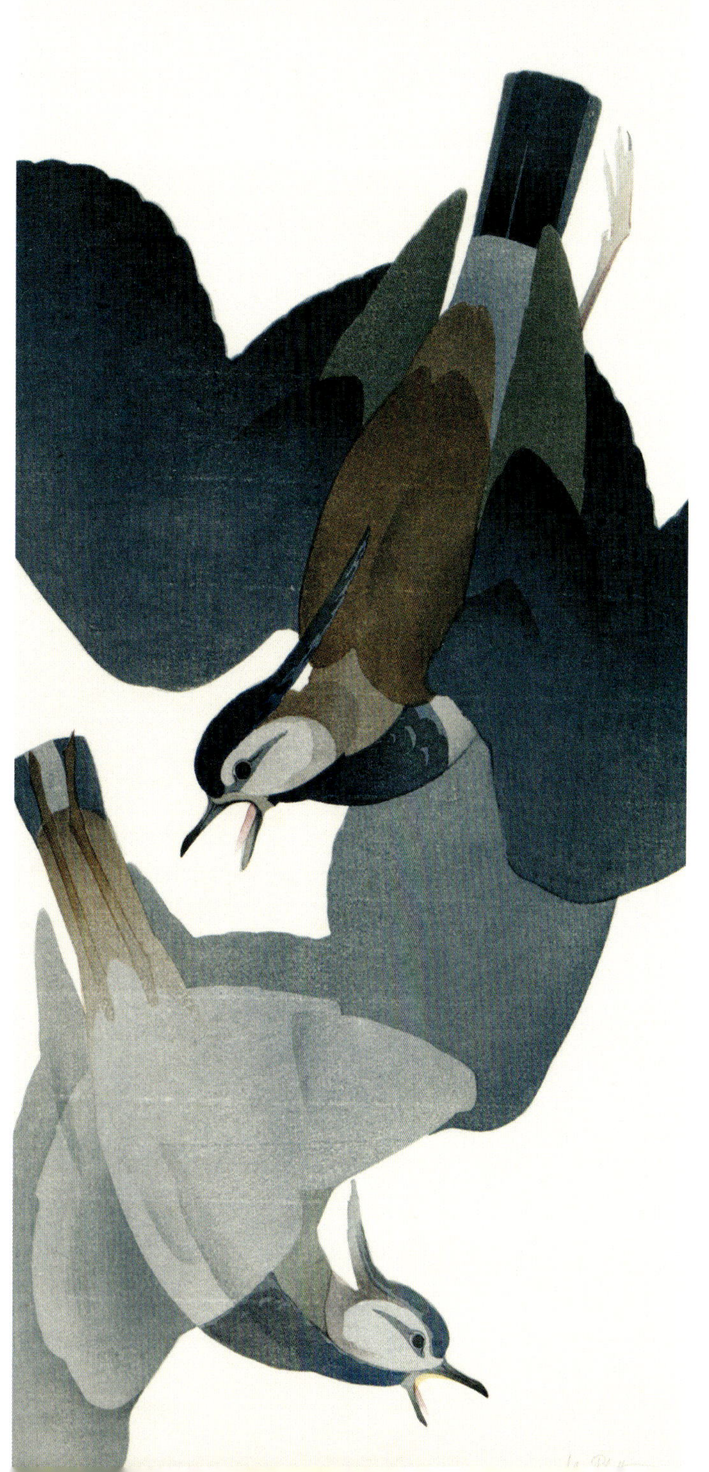

33 / *The Plough*

March 1937 / each panel 366 x 216 mm*

Triptych printed on three separate sheets.
Printed in several different colour versions
on Japanese paper, with no key block. Eight
experimental prints identified by Platt in
his printing notes thus: **i.** printed in cobalt
and ink; **ii.** as 'i'. but darker; **iii.** mostly ink,
blue in water, red in eye; **iv.** animals ink,
snowblue, red here and there; **v.** animals light
red, plough green, snow green; **vi.** animals
light red, plough pale green; **vii.** animals light
red, extra pink on hare, stoat and distant
hill; **viii.** animals ink, plough red, snow
blue/green (identified as Platt as final state).
No projected edition (5 sets of the final state
recorded; completed 1938).

Exhibited: RA, 1938, no. 1083; SGPIC, 1937,
22nd annual exhibition, no. 62; NEAC, 1937,
no. 142.
Literature: *Art Review*, November 1938.
Collections: BM, Shrimpton and Giles
Bequest, 1950; V&A, Shrimpton and Giles
Bequest, 1949.

*Some experimental prints with centre panel
re-cut and printed to 366 x 237 mm

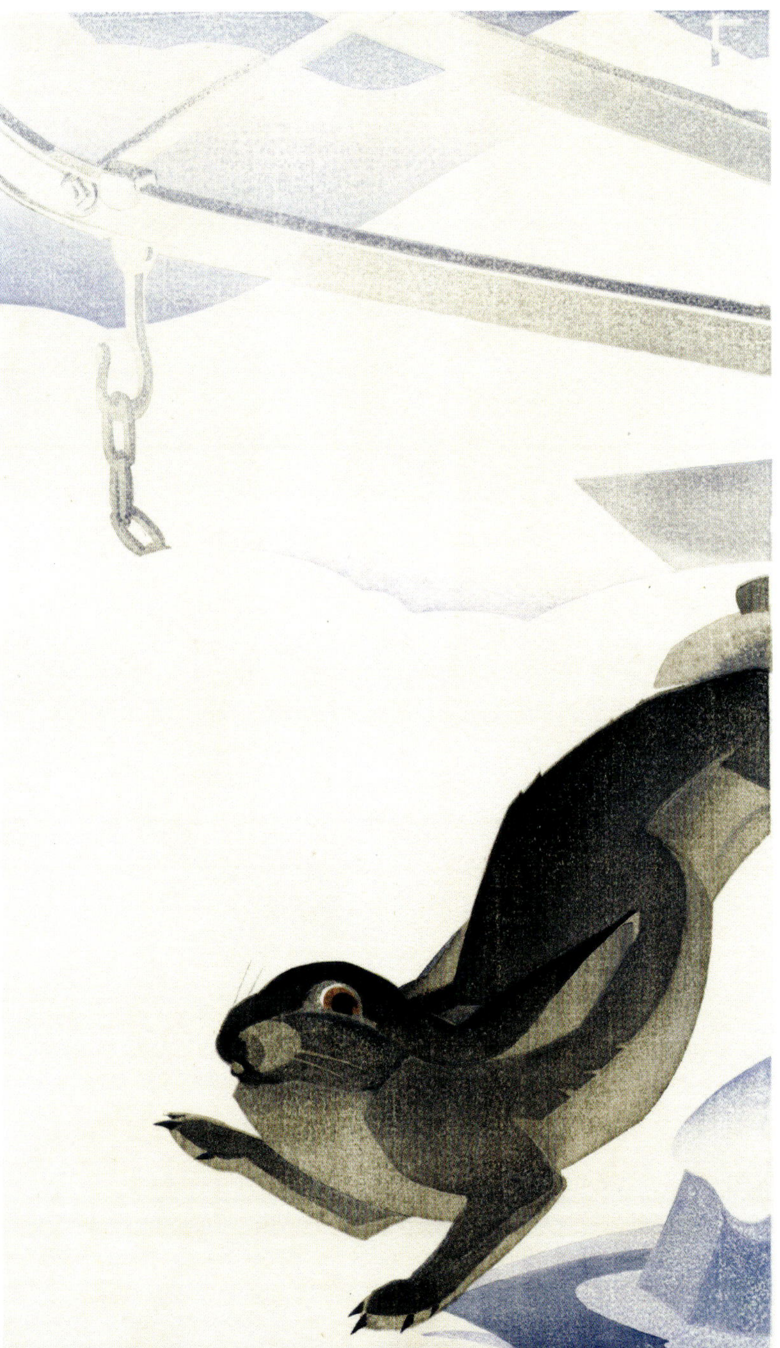

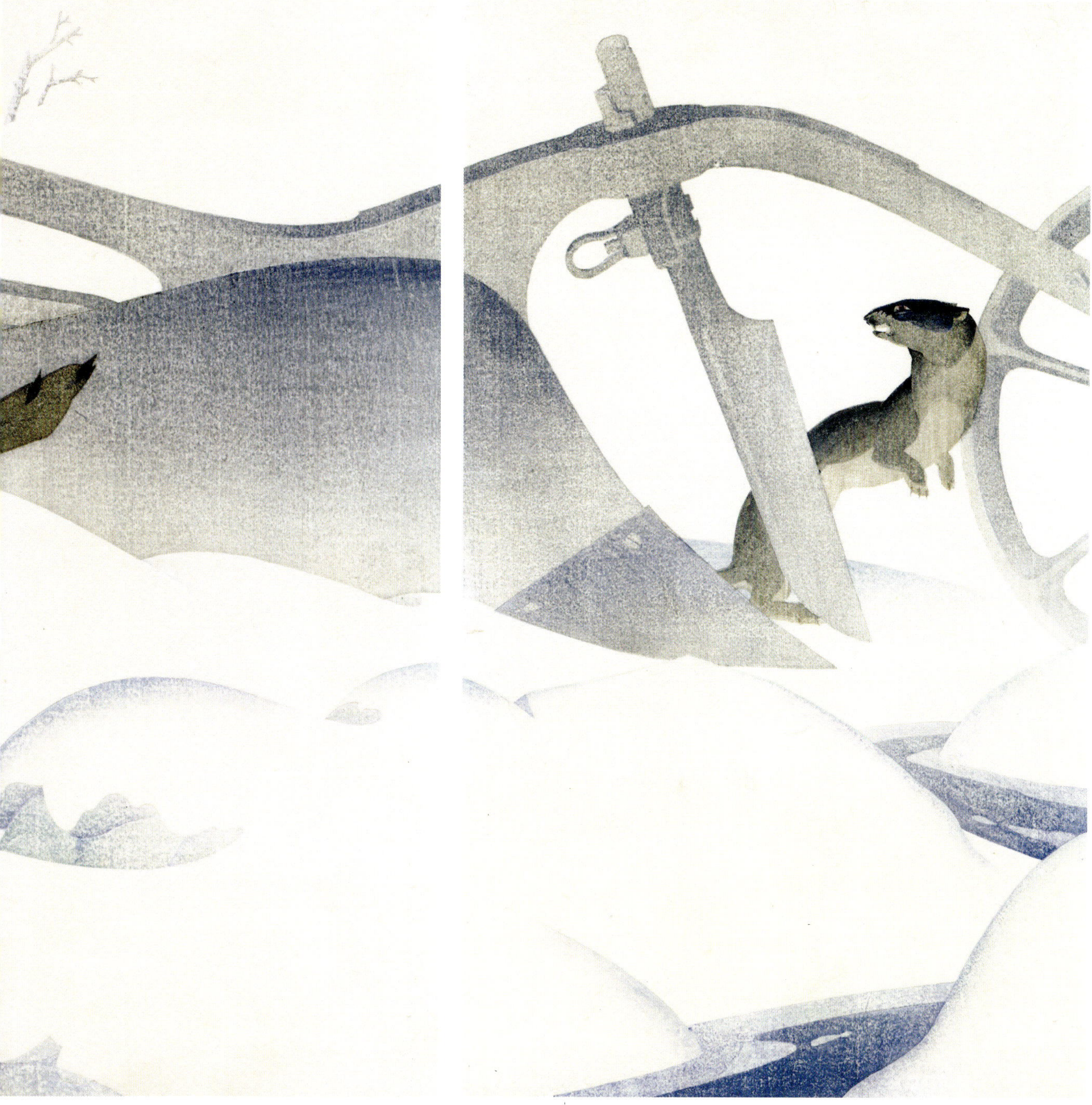

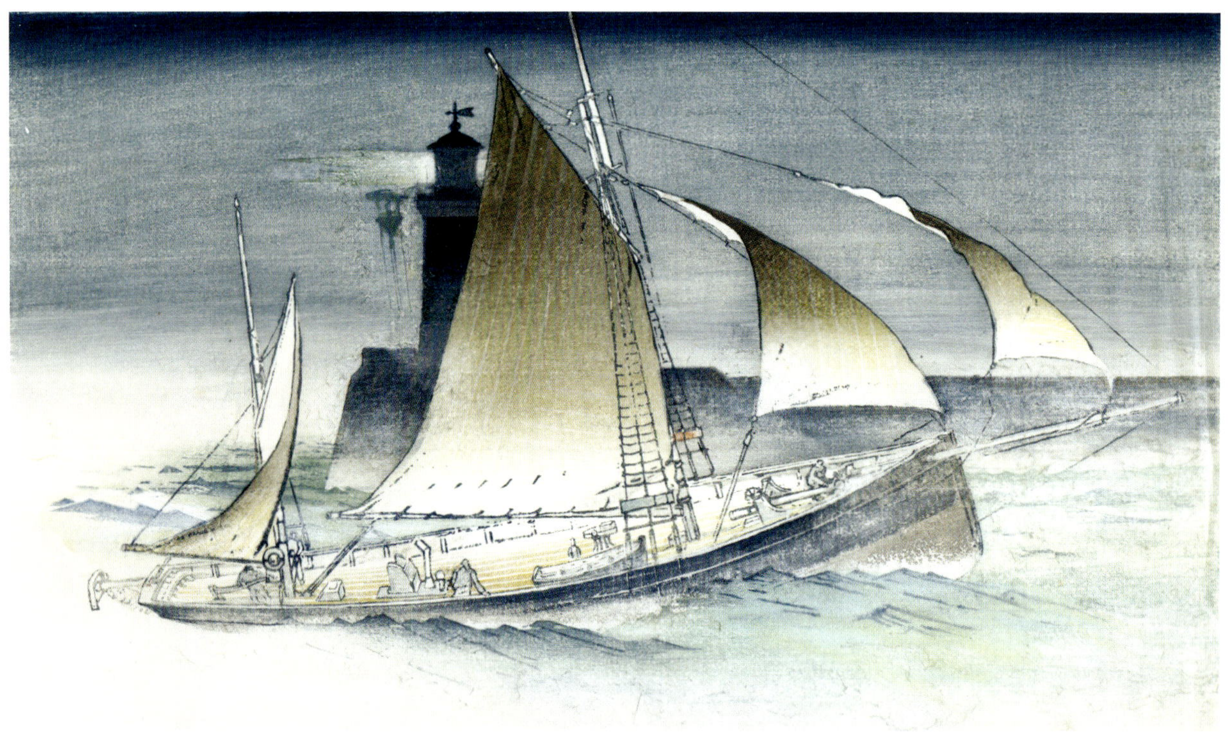

34 / *Brixham Trawler (Sailing Trawler)*

March/April 1940 / 220 x 338 mm

Printed in two colour versions on Japanese
paper, both identified by Platt as '1st state'
in his printing notes: **i**. grey, blue, dark grey
key block; **ii**. grey, blue, orange, grey key
block. No projected edition (4 recorded).
According to Platt a '2nd state' was printed
in 1947 retitled *Devon Trawler with Rainbow*.
No projected edition (3 recorded).

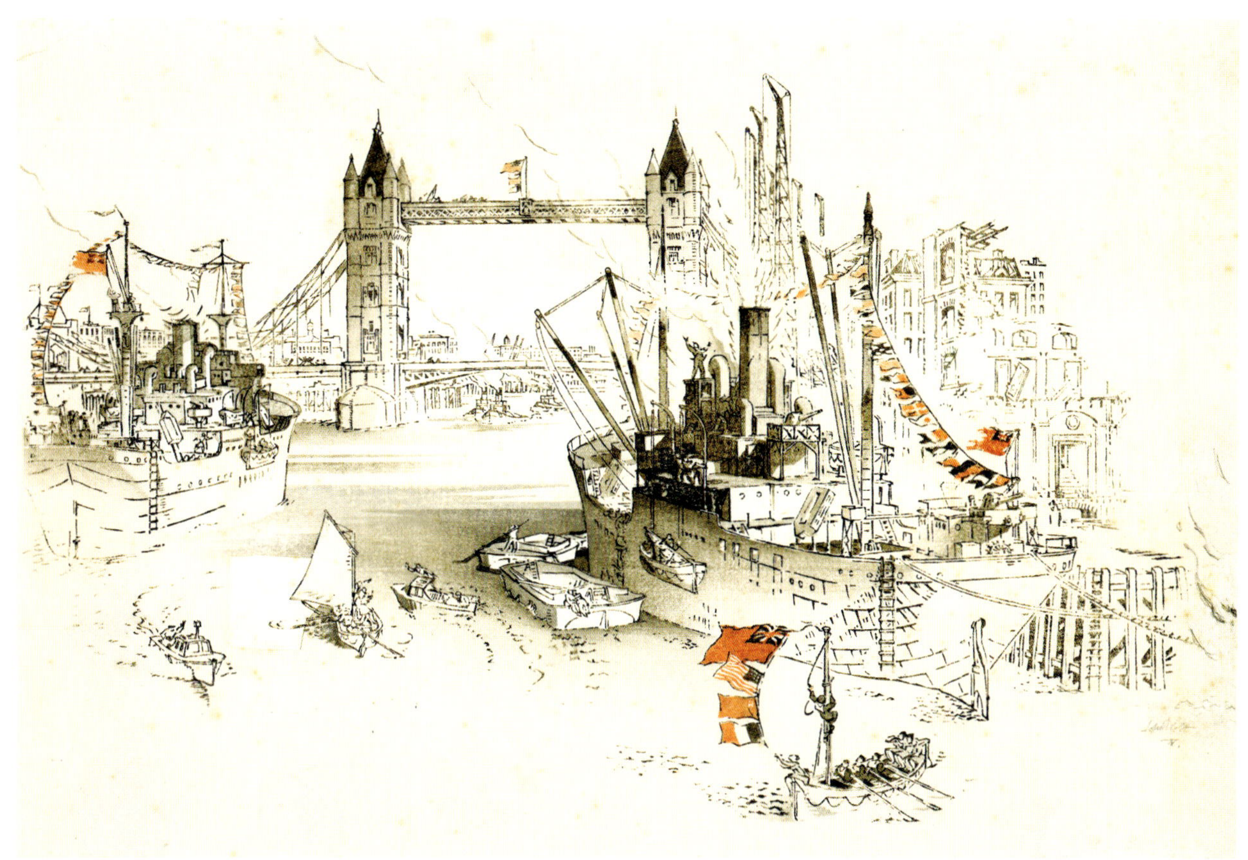

35 / *V-Day: Peace Comes to the River (Festival on the River)*

December 1945 / 235 x 364 mm

Printed in several different colour versions identified by Platt in his printing notes: **i.** outline in ink, red ensign; **ii.** printed in 1947; some with clouds, sun and rays of light added; various colour combinations in sky (yellow, red, grey ink); **iii.** printed in 1948; lemon yellow added; key block in ink; marginal line added round print; **iv.** cerulean blue outline. No projected edition (19 recorded: i–ii, numbered not recorded; iii. 4 recorded; iv. 1 recorded).

ENGRAVINGS

The following copper engravings (cats 36–40) are the only known prints made by Platt other than his colour woodcuts. Executed between 1929 and 1930 they correspond with his move to London and appointment as Principal at Blackheath School of Art. Classical in subject matter and execution, Platt's engravings illustrate his excellent draughtsmanship and are fine examples of the medium used by European artists for their original prints since the sixteenth century.

Engraving on copper entails incising an image directly into a copper plate using a sharp tool called a burin. The engraved lines of the image are filled with ink and the surface wiped clean. Paper is laid on the plate and both are passed through a press whereby the image is transferred to the paper. This is known as an intaglio printmaking process and differs from the technique of the colour woodcut in that the colour woodcut image is created in relief on the wood block and is transferred from the surface of the block onto the paper with only slight pressure.

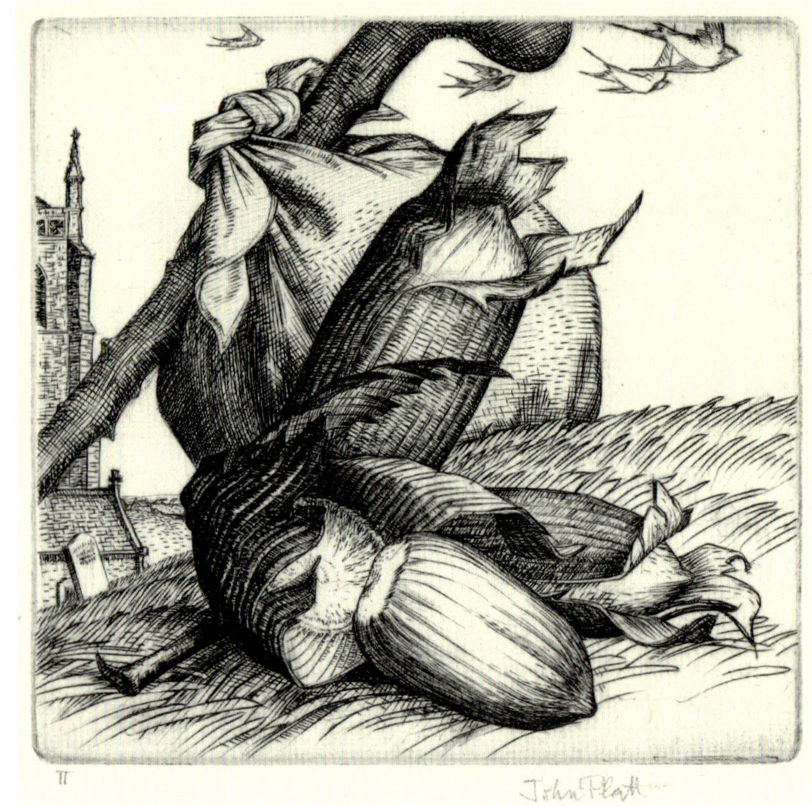

36 / *Hazelnuts*

October 1929 / 87 x 92 mm

Printed on cream laid paper, English.
Projected edition of 50 (7 recorded).

37 / *Fruit Harvest*
(*Carpent Tua Poma Nepotes*)

November 1929 / 135 x 120 mm

Printed on cream laid paper, English.
Projected edition of 100 (22 recorded).

Exhibited: RA, 1930, no. 1068.
Literature: *The Artist*, January 1937.
Collections: New Walk Museum & Art
Gallery, Leicester, acquired 1930.

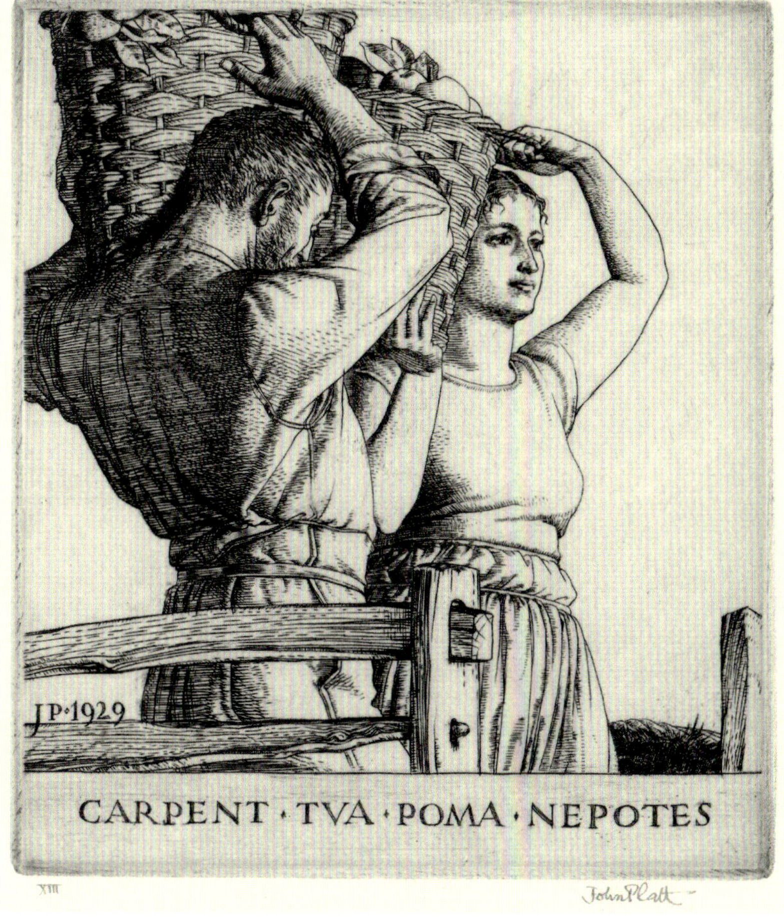

38 / *Halloween (Youth) (The Mirror)*

December 1929 / 170 x 140 mm

Printed on cream laid paper, English.
Projected edition of 100 (27 recorded).

Collections: BM, acquired 1960. Dedicated
to D. Strang the printer.

There are a few impressions (173 x 140 mm)
of a variation of this design which have a
date (1929) and a monogram in the plate (on
the side of the mirror), no fan and different
shading on the curtain.

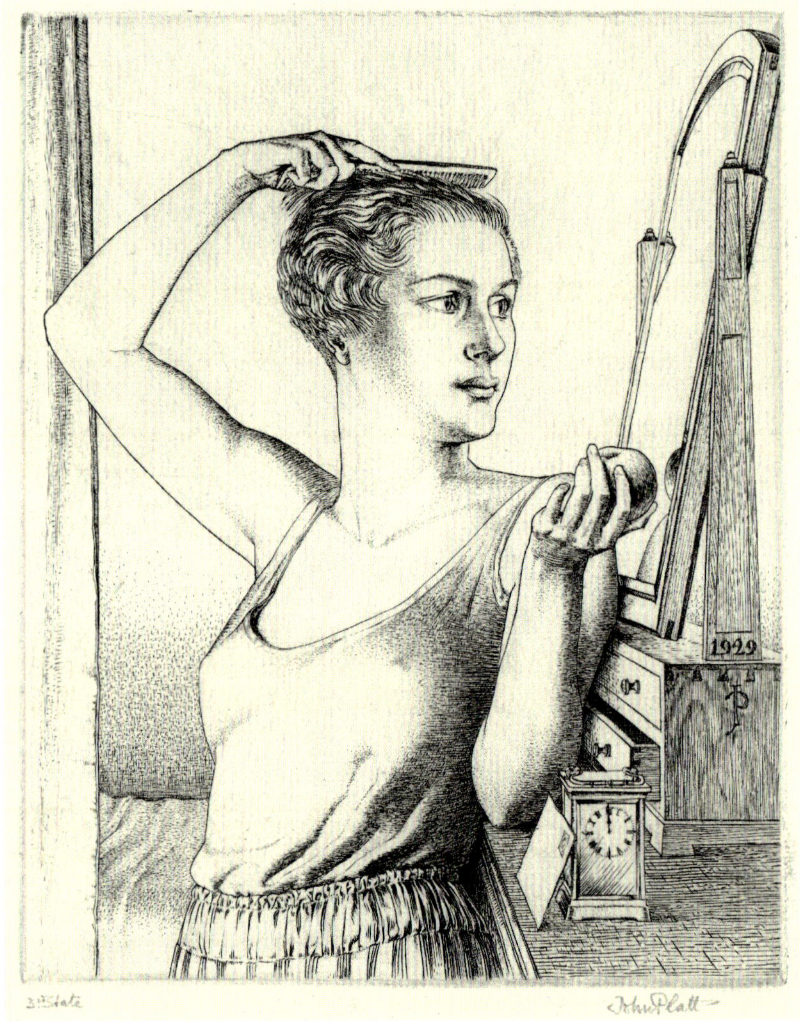

39 / *Bathers*

February/March 1930 / 162 x 138 mm

Printed on cream laid paper, English.
Projected edition of 100 (7 recorded. Plus 15
working proofs identified by Platt in his notes
in four states: **i.** '1'; **ii.** 'a–e'; **iii.** 'a–e'; **iv.** 'a–d').

Exhibited: RA, 1931, no. 1197.

According to Platt this design was never
satisfactorily finished.

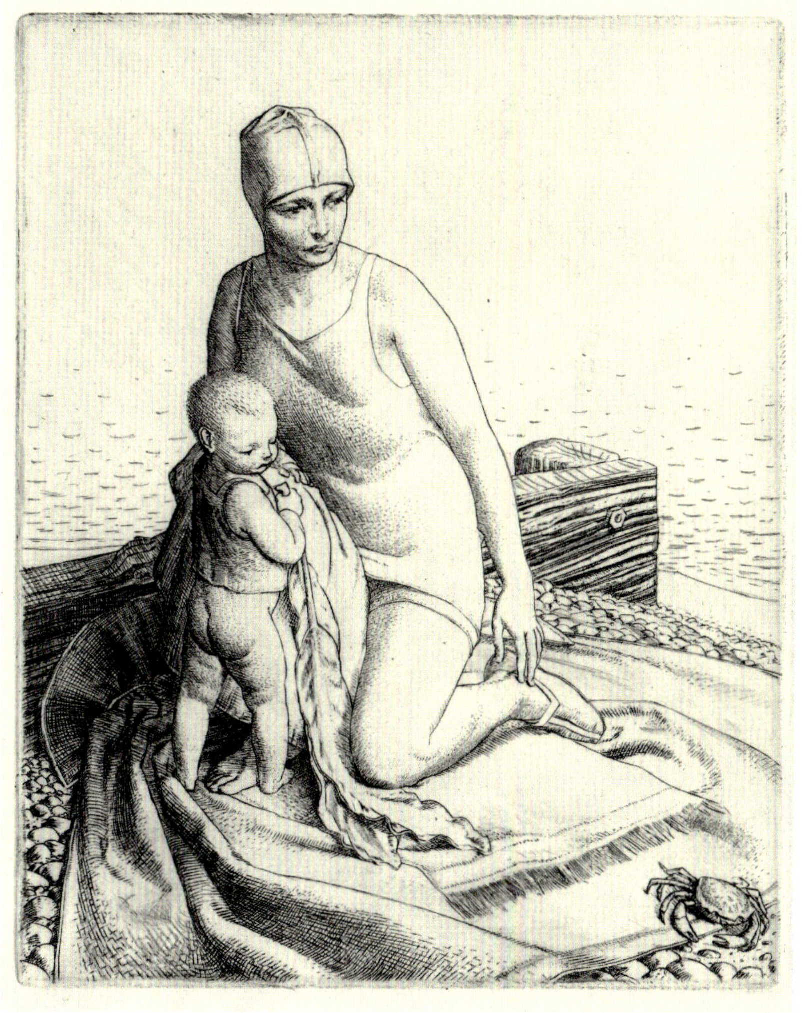

December 1930 / 190 x 140 mm

Printed on cream laid paper, English.
Projected edition of 100 (7 recorded).

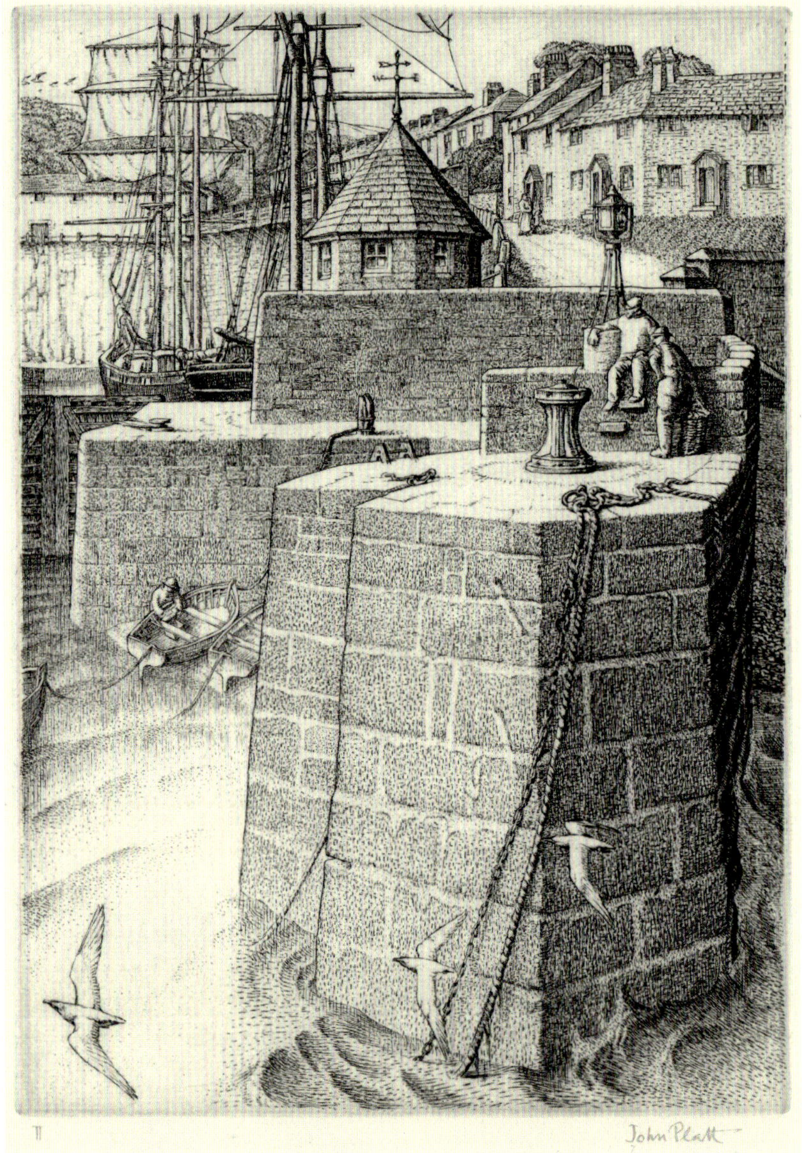

Chronology

1886–1905: Born 19 March in Leek, Staffordshire, the elder son of John Henry Platt and his wife Elizabeth (née Taylor). John Henry Platt owned the George Hotel in Leek. John Edgar, known to the family as Edgar, had two sisters, Marian and Kathleen and a brother, Sydney, who trained as an engineer and was involved in the building of a bridge over the River Ganges in India. Platt was educated at the High School Newcastle and studied briefly at Margate Art School; he intended to pursue a career as an engineer.

1903–1905: Decided to change to a career in art. His parents responded to the decision positively and offered financial support until he could manage on his own. He received a preliminary art education at Newcastle, Margate and Leek Schools of Art.

1905–1910: Awarded a scholarship in 1905 to study at the Royal College of Art, London. He received prizes in design, painting, architecture and modelling. He also studied various crafts including mural painting, stained glass, poster and book production, tapestry design, metal work and jewellery, lettering and illuminating, wood carving and architectural woodwork.

1908: Awarded Associate of The Royal College of Art in Design.

1909: Awarded Full Associate of The Royal College of Art, ARCA.

1910–1919: Principal at Leek College of Art.

1911: 24 June, married Phyllis Harvey-George. Phyllis had also been a scholar at the Royal College of Art.

1912: 31 July, daughter Anthea born.

c.1913–1916: Commissions for decorations for the Lady Chapel at All Saints Church, Leek, stained glass windows (*Miriam, Esther, Ruth*); painted decorations (*The Expulsion from Eden, The promise to Noah*); painted panelling and ceiling, painted organ case (*Raventius Fortunatus*).

1914: 29 September, son Michael born (he was also to become an artist and a scholar at the Royal College of Art). Commission for a design for a gold medal for the Leek and Moorland Co-operative Society. Other commercial commissions around this time included a cup in gilding metal, silver and enamel and silver chain.

1914–1918: War service, commission R.A.S.C. (Motor Transport).

1919–1920: Principal at Harrogate School of Art.

1920: May–October, Principal at School of Art, Derby.

1920–1923: Head of Department of Applied Art, Edinburgh College of Art, a part-time appointment.

1922: Designed poster (*For the Zoo: Alight at Camden Town or Regents Park Station*) for London Underground Electric Railway Co.

1923–1929: Principal at Leicester College of Art.

1927: Commission for the City Libraries Bookplate (Leicester).

1928: Member of the Society of Graver-Printers in Colour.

1929–1939: Principal of Blackheath School of Art, London. A part-time appointment to enable him to continue with his own work.

1934: Published a series of articles in *The Artist* (March–September).

1938: Isaac Pitman published his handbook, *Colour Woodcuts: A book of reproductions and a handbook of method.*

1938–1953: President of the Society of Graver-Printers in Colour. He put great effort into reviving the Society after the war and contributed prints to a major exhibition held by the Society at Kensington Art Gallery in 1948, 'Fifty Years of the Colour Print'.

1942: Moved to Swan Studios, Deodar Road, Putney, London.

1943–1945: Official war artist to Ministry of War Transport with numerous commissions.

1949: His wife, Phyllis, died unexpectedly and Platt's own health deteriorated. He eventually moved to Eastbourne to live with his daughter Anthea. Very little work was accomplished after 1950.

1967: 29 April, died at Eastbourne.

Notes

John Edgar Platt and the British colour woodcut

1. Artists at the The Grosvenor School of Art between the two World Wars worked in the new medium of colour linocut and produced prints which celebrated the speed, movement and energy of the modern world and were stylistically associated with Futurism.

2. Walter Crane (1845–1915) was an illustrator and important figure in the Arts and Crafts Movement. He fostered an interest in Japanese prints and the techniques by which they were produced to his pupils at Manchester School of Art at the beginning of the twentieth century.

3. Frank Morley Fletcher, *Woodblock Printing: A description of the craft of woodcutting and colour printing based on the Japanese practice*, London: J. Hogg, 1916. Allen W. Seaby, *Colour printing with linoleum and woodblocks*, Leicester: Dryad Handicrafts, 1925.

4. See, Martin Hopkinson, *No Day Without a Line: The History of the Royal Society of Painter-Printmakers 1880–1999*, Oxford, 1999, p. 30.

5. For an account of the formation of the SGPIC see, Hilary Chapman, 'John Edgar Platt and the Society of Graver-Printers in Colour', *Print Quarterly*, vol. XX, no. 2, 2003, p. 154.

6. Quoted in *The Artist*, January 1937, p. 153.

7. Platt's note books and edition books were donated to the Prints and Drawings Department at the British Museum, 1999.

8. *The Times*, 29 May 1967.

9. Quoted in G.M. Ellwood, 'Famous Contemporary Art Masters', *Drawing and Design*, November 1924, p. 186.

10. John Platt, *Colour woodcuts: A book of reproductions and a handbook of method*, London: Sir Isaac Pitman and Sons Ltd., 1938.

11. *Original Colour Print Magazine*, William Giles (ed.), published 1924, 1925, 1926. *The Colour Print Club Journal*, William Giles (ed.), published 1931, 1933.

12. Letter from Henry Hayley to John Platt in the Platt archive, 18 September 1939.

The influence of Yoshijiro Urushibara

1. For information on Yoshijiro Urushibara and a catalogue of his works see Hilary Chapman and Libby Horner, *Yoshijiro Urushibara: A Japanese printmaker in London*, Leiden, The Netherlands: Brill Publishers, 2017.

2. This handpainted scroll, is signed by the fourth-century Chinese artist Gu Kaizhi and depicted a series of scenes intended as an instruction manual on correct behaviour for the ladies of the imperial harem.

3. *Bruges* portfolio published by the Morland Press, 1919 (edition of 50). Contents include: a sheet with an introduction by Paul Lambotte CBE, Director General des Beaux Arts de Belgique; six large (40 x 50 cm) colour woodcuts by Yoshijiro Urushibara after designs by Frank Brangwyn; six pages with a poem by Lawrence Binyon; a colour woodcut headpiece by Urushibara after a design by Frank Brangwyn.

4. Lawrence Binyon, introduction to *Ten Woodcuts cut and printed in Colour by Yoshijiro Urushibara after Designs by Frank Brangwyn RA*, portfolio published by John Lane, the Bodley Head (edition of 250).

5. Letters to Platt from Henry Hayley in the Platt archive, c. 1940.

Bibliography

Books

Chapman, Hilary and Horner, Libby: *Yoshijiro Urushibara: A Japanese printmaker in London*, Leiden, The Netherlands: Brill Publishers, 2017.

Garton, Robin (ed.), *British Printmakers 1855–1955; A century of British printmaking from the etching revival to St. Ives*, Garton and Co., in association with Scolar Press, 1922.

Ingles, G.S., *The Arms of the City of Leicester* (a book proposed and initiated by Platt, it contains his essay, 'Notes on Heraldic Design', and woodcut, *The City Libraries*), 1932.

Morley Fletcher, Frank, *Woodblock Printing: A description of the craft of woodcutting and colour printing based on the Japanese practice*, J. Hogg: London, 1916.

Platt, John Edgar, *Colour Woodcuts: A book of reproductions and a handbook of method*, Isaac Pitman, 1938.

Seaby, Allen W., *Colour Printing with Linoleum and Woodblocks*, Dryad Handicrafts: Leicester, 1925.

Articles and reviews

Bliss, Douglas Percy, 'Prints and Drawings', *Art Review*, 15 November 1938, p. 39.

Chapman, Hilary, 'John Edgar Platt and and the Society of Graver Printers in Colour', *Print Quarterly*, vol. xx, no. 2, 2003, pp. 145–158.

Ellwood, G.M., 'Famous Contemporary Art Masters – John Platt', *Drawing and Design*, vol. 4, new series VI, November 1924. pp. 185–191.

Fletcher, Frank Morley, 'The Work of John Platt', *The Studio*, vol. 90, no. 392, November 1925, p. 297.

Grimsditch, Herbert B., 'Artists of Note, no. 23, John Platt', *The Artist*, January 1937, p. 150.

Journal of National Society of Art Masters (a review of *Colour Woodcuts*), vol. X, no. 8, May 1938.

Platt, John Edgar, 'Notes on Colour Woodblock Printing', *The Studio*, vol. 90, no. 392, November 1925, p. 281.

Platt, John Edgar, 'Colour Woodcuts', *The Artist* (seven articles, one each month), March–September 1934.

Salaman, Malcolm C., 'Modern Woodcuts and Lithographs by British and French artists', *The Studio* (special number), p. 32, 1919.

'Studio Talk', *The Studio*, vol. 72, 1917, pp. 160–161.

The Studio, vol. 83, no. 348, March 1922, p.163.

The Studio, vol. 89, no. 385, April 1925, p. 223.

The Studio, vol. 105, no. 478, January 1933.

The Times (obituary), 29 May 1967.

Collections

Paintings and prints by John Edgar Platt are included in the collections of the following museums, art galleries and institutions:

Belfast: Ulster Museum
Doncaster: Doncaster Museum and Art Gallery
Hereford: Hereford Museum and Art Gallery
Leicester: New Walk Museum & Art Gallery (formerly Leicester City Art Gallery and Museum)
London: British Museum; Imperial War Museum; National Maritime Museum; Tate; Victoria and Albert Museum
Manchester: Manchester Art Gallery; Whitworth Art Gallery
Oldham: Gallery Oldham
Southport: The Atkinson

Canada: Vancouver Art Gallery
Germany: Gutenberg Museum, Mainz
Russia: The Pushkin State Museum of Fine Arts, Moscow
USA: The Metropolitan Museum of Art, New York; California State Library; Museum of Fine Arts, Boston

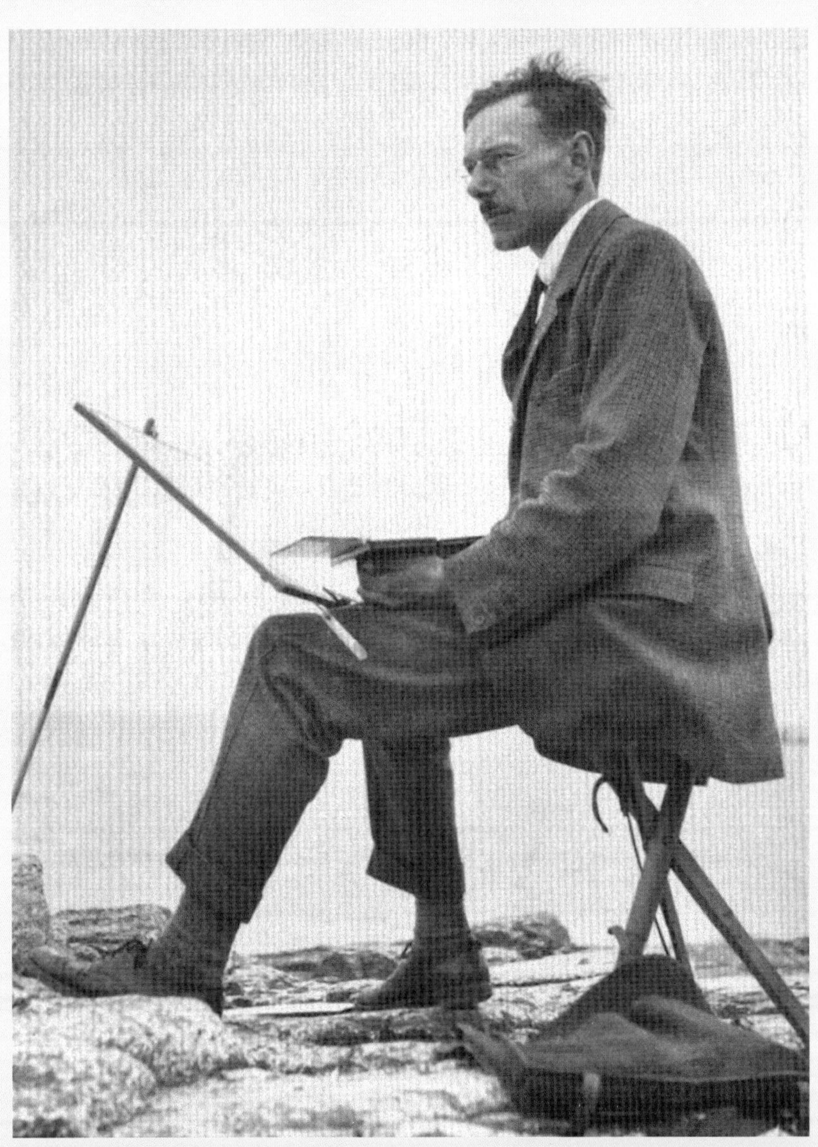

Index

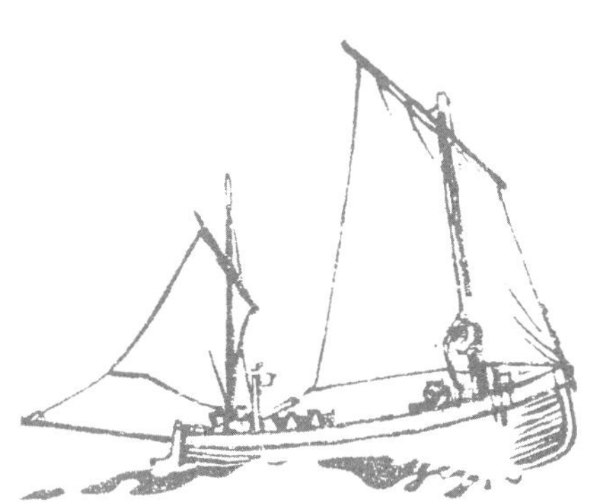